Why not Embroider Boxes?

Daphne J Ashby
&
Jackie Woolsey

August 2003

DEDICATION
We should like to dedicate this book to the staff at Keely Print,
in particular Martin and Malcolm, who have always been so patient and
helpful in guiding us through every stage in the production of our books.

Other books by the same authors:

Ribbon Embroidery
>published by David & Charles, Newton Abbott
>Hardback - September 1996, Paperback - August 1998

Creative Embroidery Techniques using Colour through Gold
>published by the Guild of Master Craftsman Publications Ltd.
>Lewes - June 1998

Why not make a Beaded Amulet Purse?
>self-published - June 1998

Why not Carry on Beading?
>self-published - June 1999

Stumpwork - Why Not?
>self-published - January 2001

Why not Embroider Letters?
>self-published - January 2002

Why not make a Box? (by Jackie)
>self-published - September 1996

Making Hand-Sewn Boxes (by Jackie)
>published by the Guild of Master Craftsman Publications Ltd.
>Lewes - April 1999

Copyright 20

This

CONTENTS

INTRODUCTION

When we first met, more than a decade ago, Daphne was already a well-known embroiderer, I was making fabric-covered boxes and we were both busy teaching and lecturing on our individual subjects. Since then, through working and publishing books together on various needle-based subjects, we have gradually expanded our interests - probably beyond either of our original horizons - but also combined our skills.

In a magazine article, we were once described as "chalk and cheese", which is very accurate insofar as we are, happily, entirely non-competitive in what we do, either together or separately, but I have learned a great deal from Daphne's patient instruction.

Much of the success of our co-operation in writing books is due to our very different approaches to publishing. Once we have decided that we think we can bring a fresh approach to a subject (we have never sat down "to write a book" but the ideas have just evolved), Daphne gets on with some creative stitching whilst I sit at the computer, working out the possible schedule and content. However, once we have got going and Daphne sends me each creation and instructions, I question every detail and we send the print-outs back and forth until I am quite sure that I can understand everything. Only then do the draft, charts, photographs, etc., become the final version.

This book brings us full circle, so to speak, and is a perfect product of our writing partnership - Daphne's embroidery and my boxes. All of the boxes are new designs and none appeared in my previous book on "Making Hand-Sewn Boxes" and some have been provoked by a phrase that I have become used to hearing from Daphne: "I've seen this box - I'm sure you could design and make one like it!".

My methods for box-making have not changed and, should you not tackled the craft before, the book's first few sections will the basic techniques for creating fabric-c instructions for making the new boxes, fo ideas for embellishing your boxes, rangir embroidery to ribbon, stumpwork, beadin "Colour through Gold".

We both hope that you will read, learn an embroidering boxes.

1

FIRST THINGS FIRST

PLEASE read these important notes before starting any of the projects

EMBROIDERY

When using Congress Cloth and "counting" for stitches, please note that you need to bring the needle up through a hole and then count. This way you can count either threads or holes, whichever you find easier.

Dimensions for embroidery, frames, etc., are expressed in imperial measurements.

BOXES

Dimensions for card cutting are shown in millimetres. It is possible to achieve more accurate measurements using the metric scale and imperial equivalents are not practical.

The use of cotton or polycotton is assumed and allowance has been made for this weight of fabric. If heavier fabrics are used, it will be necessary to make additional allowances.

As each stage of a box is completed, check that the cut card for the next stage is accurate before lacing.

When cutting out fabric, a margin allowance of 20mm is approximately ¾", 25mm is about 1" and 30mm about 1¼".

MATERIALS AND EQUIPMENT REQUIRED FOR BOX-MAKING

Complicated or costly equipment is not required and most of the items listed will probably be readily available in the home.

The thick card used in the construction of most fabric-covered boxes is 2mm greyboard (sometimes referred to as strawboard), which is the type of card used by framers as backing for photographs, etc. Craft suppliers and art shops will probably be the best source of supply. More often than not, off-cuts will suffice, since the individual pieces required are not large. Do not confuse this thick card with mounting board, which is not really strong enough for making the boxes described in this book.

The thin card, which is used as lining for some boxes, can be cut from cereal or other packaging, which is just the right weight.   (Never throw any more thin card away from now on - perfect "recycling".)

An HB Pencil with a good, sharp point.

Ruler - A wooden or plastic ruler with well-defined markings, as accurate measuring is essential when ruling the dimensions for boxes.

Set square or protractor - It is very important that right angles really are 90°
to ensure that pieces of card fit together properly and finished boxes are well shaped.

Knife - it cannot be stressed too strongly how vital it is to have a really sharp blade for cutting the card.   Since the greyboard is quite thick, a Stanley knife with a new blade is ideal for the purpose.   The lighter-weight craft knives will suffice but will require firm pressure and a little more patience.   Replace the blades frequently as they will blunt quite quickly.

Metal ruler - Always use the knife against a metal edge when cutting.   The purchase of a metal safety ruler will prove a very sound investment and could save tears and possible bloodshed.   (Never attempt to cut card guided by a wooden or plastic ruler, which can be dangerous and will ruin the ruler.)

Cutting surface - this is used as a protection for the surface beneath the card when cutting.   This can be a sufficiently large piece of wood or plastic or, ideally, one of the purpose-made special cutting mats, which have "self-healing" surfaces and have been developed especially for this purpose.

<u>Strong thread</u> for lacing can be any linen, nylon or polyester thread, or even thin crochet cotton, which does not break under tension.

<u>Padding</u> - Practically any thin wadding, foam, felt (even strips of blanket) can be used to pad the sides and lids of boxes.   The thickness of the padding depends entirely on the effect you wish to achieve.

<u>Sewing kit</u> - Just a few basic sewing items are required: threads to match/tone with your chosen fabrics, large scissors for cutting out and finer ones for the sewing techniques.

<u>Needles</u>: Large-eyed needle for lacing
Sharps, etc., for ordinary sewing
Curved needle for joining fabric-covered surfaces

The <u>curved needle</u> should be as fine as possible and the smallest you can comfortably handle for the best results. (Fine curved needle No. FNC15 may be found suitable for the purpose.)   Achieving a neat finish when making boxes is certainly helped by the use of a curved needle and time spent mastering the technique of handling it will bring its own reward.

<u>Double-sided self-adhesive tape</u> is used when making an aperture in a frame for insetting an embroidery.

<u>Needlework finisher</u> (or similar 'fray check, e.g. thin PVA glue) is helpful to minimise the possibility of fraying when cutting apertures in fabric - check that it will not stain the fabric (try a spot in an obscure place and allow to dry) before use.

There is really no restriction on the types of <u>fabrics</u> that can be used for making boxes, although undoubtedly the fine cottons and polycottons are the easiest to handle and give highly satisfactory results.   It is possible, however, to use silks, furnishing fabrics, dupion, corduroy, velvet and thin leathers.   Making boxes is also an excellent way of using small left-over lengths of fabrics which have been used for curtains, bed covers, cushions, upholstery, etc., which will also provide another element of co-ordination in room furnishing.

N.B. Always try to cut along the straight grain of the fabric.

If you are embellishing your box and/or its lid with embroidery, beads, ribbons, etc., then choose the outer fabric for the box with care to co-ordinate with the style and colours used in the decoration.

BASIC TECHNIQUES

Planning

Before starting on the construction of a box, it is important to plan the details: size, shape, divisions, lid stays, risers, trays, drawers, etc. If the box is to involve any form of embroidery or other needlework, this should also be thought about before making the box. It is to this aspect of planning that much of this book is devoted, giving many ideas for the decoration of boxes.

Marking the greyboard

It is important to rule out and mark accurately in pencil the dimensions of the box you are going to make. Ensure that all the corners are right angles, that is 90 degrees, by using a set square or protractor to check each one. Always double-check the dimensions carefully before starting to cut the card.

Cutting the card

Cut the card carefully along the pencil lines, using a Stanley or similar knife, held against a metal edge with a cutting surface beneath.

Position the metal edge on the pencil line and, holding the knife against it, draw the blade steadily towards you with firm but gentle pressure, repeating the stroke until the card is cut through.

The indentation made by the pencil will provide a groove which will help to keep the knife in position on the first stroke and, thereafter, the blade will follow the previous cut if steady pressure is maintained.

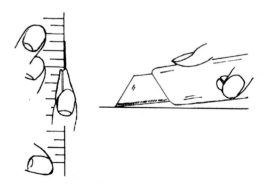

Cutting card with a Stanley knife against a metal edge

As each piece of card is marked out, write the dimensions on it in pencil - it is so easy to become confused when several pieces of card are being cut out at the same time, especially if they are similar in size. This is also important if there are several people cutting out card for making boxes.

Chamfering

When cutting card where very precise corners are important, e.g. when making risers and/or trays, it can be advantageous to chamfer the edges of the card to make the pieces fit together very closely at the corners. This is achieved by holding the knife at an acute angle and cutting along the edge of the card.

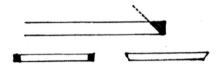

Chamfering card

Lacing fabric over card

This is a sewing method of covering card with fabric. Cut the fabric to be laced larger all round than the card to be covered. This margin varies in size and is detailed in the text referring to each box.

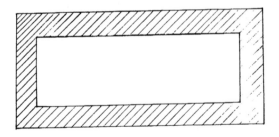

Card on fabric showing margin

Use strong thread, e.g. linen, nylon, polyester, etc., for lacing, which enables the fabric to be tensioned to achieve a wrinkle-free surface. By threading the needle and rather than cutting off a length, leaving the thread attached to the reel until the lacing has been carried the full length of the fabric being laced, it is possible to tension the lacing by working backwards and avoids having to join the thread.

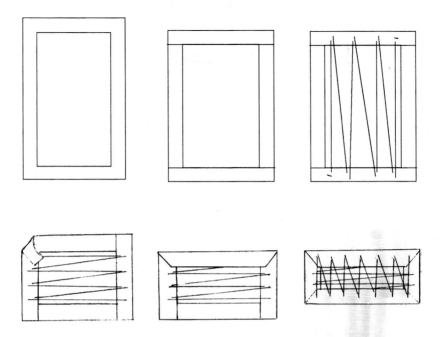

Sequence for lacing the fabric over a rectangular piece of card

Using a curved needle

The efficient use of a curved needle enables two flat fabric-covered surfaces to be joined together invisibly. Ladder stitch is employed but the curved needle makes this a simpler operation.

Curved needle in use

Stitching side pieces to the base card for a padded box

When making a padded box, the covered card pieces are oversewn together. Place one fabric-covered piece of side card face to face with one edge of the covered base and sew the edges together through the fabric, as shown in the following diagrams:

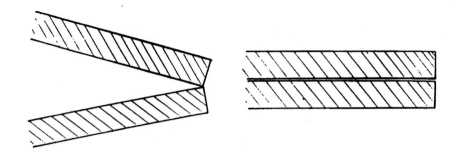

Placing card faces together and prior to oversewing

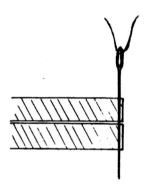

Stitching card faces together

<u>Stitching side pieces to the base card for a double-layer box</u>

For this type of box, pieces of fabric-covered card are stitched together at right angles to each other and this involves the use of a curved needle and ladder stitch.

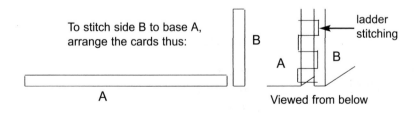

Stitching two pieces of fabric-covered card together at right angles

Ladder stitch

This stitch is used to join two flat surfaces together more or less invisibly. Take a stitch in one fabric and a stitch in the second fabric immediately in line with the first stitch and continue this process.

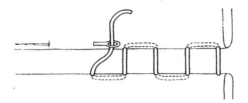

Ladder stitch

Identifying parts of a box

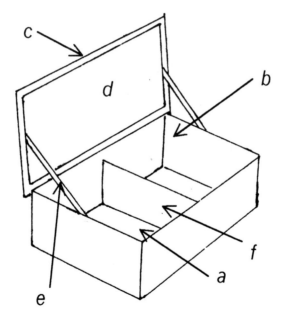

a Base
b Side
c Lid
d Lid liner
e Stay
f Divider

LID FINISHES

INSERTING A RECTANGULAR PANEL INTO A LID

Always ensure that there will be a margin of at least 25mm around the embroidery when the panel has been inserted.

On the piece of card which has been selected for the lid, mark an outline with the dimensions of the finished embroidery. Using a Stanley knife with a sharp blade, carefully cut out this rectangle and, if necessary, remove any rough edges with a sanding block. Place the card on a piece of padding cut to the same dimensions and draw the outline of the rectangle onto the padding. Cut out this piece of padding and retain.

Cut a piece of outer fabric to cover the piece of card, allowing a margin of 30mm all round. Place the card centrally on the wrong side of the fabric and draw the outline of the inner rectangle on the fabric in pencil.

Paint needlework finisher (or similar fray check) along the pencil line on the fabric and allow to dry. (Always try the fray check first on a spare piece of fabric to check that it will not stain.) Cut out a rectangle of fabric 20mm inside the pencil line and then cut up to the line at intervals.

Position pieces of double-sided tape on the lid card all round the cut out panel. Place the outer fabric, right side down, on a firm surface with the padding in position on top and then the piece of card, lining up the rectangular holes.

Lid card, with double-sided tape around the aperture, positioned on the fabric

Remove the paper from the double-sided adhesive tape and carefully pull the fabric evenly through the hole in the padding and card and press onto the adhesive tape.

From the right side, position the completed embroidered panel behind the covered/padded rectangular cut-out, ensuring that the design is central. Turn the lid over, keeping the embroidery in place, and position the rectangle of padding over the panel into the recess, which will give the embroidered panel a raised effect.   Hold these in position with masking tape.

Pin one pair of opposite sides of the lid fabric, pulling the fabric firmly and evenly to remove any creases, and lace, keeping the lacing stitches well away from the edges - this is to ensure that the lacing stitches will not show when the lid lining is stitched into position.   Pin and lace the other two sides, mitring the corners carefully - they will be visible on the underside of the completed lid.

Position the covered lid lining card centrally on the underside of the covered lid, laced surfaces together, and stitch into place all round the edge of the lining card.

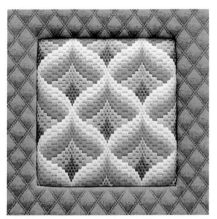

Embroidered panel inserted in a lid

INSERTING AN EMBROIDERY INTO A CIRCULAR FRAME

Using a Stanley knife with a sharp blade, carefully mark and cut out a circle of the same dimensions as the embroidery on the lid card and, if necessary, remove any rough edges with a sanding block.

Cut a piece of padding the same size as the lid card and draw the outline of the circle on to the padding.   Cut out this circle of padding and retain.

Cut a piece of outer fabric to cover the lid card, allowing a margin of 30mm all round.   Place the card centrally on the wrong side of the fabric and draw the outline of the circle on the fabric in pencil.

Paint needlework finisher (or similar fray check, eg. PVA glue) along the pencil line, allow to dry, and then cut out a circle of fabric 15mm inside this line, and cut up to the outline at intervals as shown below.

N.B. If using fray check (it is not essential) always try it on a spare piece of fabric first to make sure that it will not leave a mark when dry.

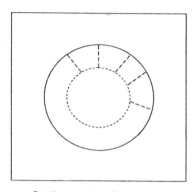

Cutting out the fabric circle

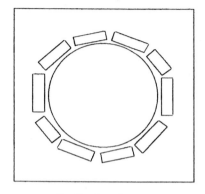

Positioning the tape

Position pieces of double-sided tape as shown above.

Place the outer fabric, right side down, on a firm surface with the padding in position on top and then the piece of thick card, lining up the circular holes in each. Remove the paper from the double-sided adhesive tape and carefully pull the fabric evenly through the hole in the padding and card and press onto the adhesive tape.

From the right side, position the completed embroidered panel behind the covered/padded circular cut-out, ensuring that the design is central. Turn the lid over, keeping the embroidery in place, and position the circle of padding over the panel into the recess, which will give the embroidered panel a raised effect. Hold these in position with masking tape.

Pin one pair of opposite sides of the lid fabric, pulling the fabric firmly and evenly to remove any creases, and lace, keeping the lacing stitches well away from the edges - this is to ensure that the lacing stitches will not show when the lid lining is stitched into position. Pin and lace the other two sides, mitring the corners carefully - they will be visible on the underside of the completed lid.

Position the covered lid lining card centrally on the underside of the covered lid, laced surfaces together, and stitch into place all round the edge of the lining card.

EMBELLISHING A LID

Stitching a panel worked on Congress Cloth to a lid using ribbon and beads

Carefully trim the Congress Cloth to within four threads of the embroidered panel and position in the centre of a piece of box lining fabric sufficient to cover the piece of card on which the embroidery is to be mounted.

Pin and tack lengths of gold ribbon on each side of the embroidery, covering the Congress Cloth edge and overlapping at the corners as shown in the diagram and photographs below.

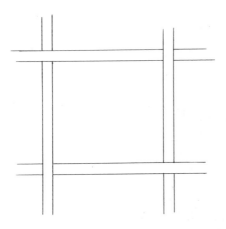

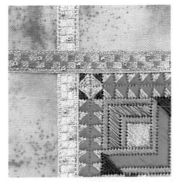 

Gold ribbon surrounding the embroidery

Stitch the ribbons into place using small gold beads, in a zig-zag pattern along each length. Patterned ribbon can help with the positioning of the beads. Cut a piece of padding to the exact dimensions of the piece of card and, carefully centralising the embroidery, lace the fabric over the padding and card.

Cut a piece of greyboard for the finished lid and lace it with a piece of the outer covering fabric, keeping the lacing stitches well in from the edges.

Cut a piece of thin card for the lining so that, when it is stitched to the under-side of the lid, it will fit inside the box carcass when the lid is closed. Lace with lining fabric and, using ladder stitch with a curved needle, stitch it to the underside of the lid.

"Colour through Gold" panel attached to the fabric using ribbon and beads and stitched onto the lid of a napkin box

Stitching an embroidered panel onto a lid

When using other embroidery techniques on a background fabric, this can be stretched straight over a piece of card which can then be stitched, using ladder stitch and a curved needle, directly onto the covered lid card.

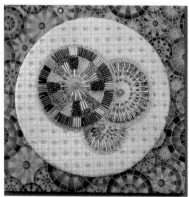

Bead-embroidered panel laced over a circular piece of card and stitched directly onto the lid of a napkin box

HINGING A LID

Place the box carcass on a firm surface, hinge on the far side, and position the lid on top with any decoration or pattern the correct way up.

Turn the box upside down on to its lid, keeping the hinge on the far side. Gently tilt the box backwards to view the hinge lying on the lid; holding this firmly, allow the base to stand vertically and then pin the hinge into position along the edge as close to the back of the box as possible. Do not remove these pins until the lid section has been completed.

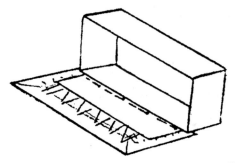

Showing a hinge being pinned into position on a lid

Position the lid lining card centrally on the lid (on top of the hinge) laced sides together, and pin into position. Check by closing the lid that it is positioned correctly and that the lining card fits inside the box when the lid is closed. If lid stays are being incorporated, pin these into position now and stitch in place with the lid lining.

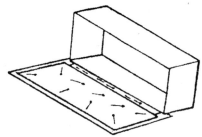

Lining pinned onto the lid, sandwiching the hinge

Ladder-stitch the lining to the lid all round the edge of the lining card, using a curved needle, being particularly careful to stitch through all layers along the hinge edge, where the needle will have to be used almost vertically. If necessary, with the box closed, stitch the underside of the back edge of the lid to the box to give additional strength.

1. SMALL SQUARE DOUBLE-LAYER BOX

This square box, the internal dimensions of which are approximately 100mm long x 100mm wide x 65mm high (4" x 4" x 2.5") is suitable for the storage of all sorts of small treasures, e.g. jewellery, needlework threads and equipment or just knick-knacks.

1.1 Basic
   small square
   double-layer box

Materials

2mm greyboard
Two fat quarters of cotton fabric
     - one patterned fabric and one plain fabric
Strong thread for lacing
Sewing thread to match/tone with fabrics
Padding for lid

Equipment

Sharp pencil, set square and ruler
Cutting mat, sharp Stanley knife and metal safety ruler
Scissors, pins and sewing needles
Fine curved needle

Preparation

Identify the pieces of card as shown in the diagram on the opposite page.

Cut out the card, following the instructions given in the Basic Techniques section, to the following dimensions:

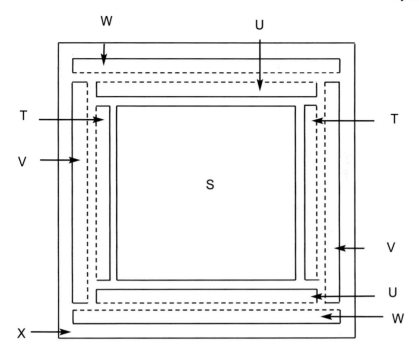

1.2   Bird's eye view of the square box on a platform base. The laced surfaces are indicated by dotted lines.

S	Inside base	100mm x 100mm	cut 1
T	Inner sides	100mm x 70mm	cut 2
U	Inner sides	106mm x 70mm	cut 2
V	Outer sides	106mm x 70mm	cut 2
W	Outer sides	112mm x 70mm	cut 2
X	Platform base	127mm x 127mm	cut 1
Y	Lid	127mm x 127mm	cut 1
Z	Lid lining	98mm x 98mm	cut 1

The lid lining can be cut from thinner card if you prefer.

<u>Method of construction</u>

Cut out lining fabric for each of the card pieces S, T (2) and U (2), allowing a margin of 20mm all round, and lace the fabric over the card.

Attach one covered side T, laced side outwards, to the covered base S, laced side downwards, stitching along the underside.   Use a matching sewing thread and ladder stitch with a curved needle.

Why not Embroider Boxes?

Stitch the second side T and the two sides U into place, in accordance with diagram 1.2. Stitch down the corners using ladder stitch with the curved needle.

Cut outer fabric, allowing a margin of 20mm all round, to cover card pieces V (2) and W (2) and lace the fabric over the card.

Position one covered side V in the correct place on the outside of the box, with the laced surface facing inwards, as shown in the bird's eye view diagram. Stitch into position along all the edges, using ladder stitch and a curved needle. Stitch the second side V into position and then add the two covered sides W, stitching these in the same way.

Platform Base:

Cut a piece of outer fabric to cover the card piece X, allowing a margin of 30mm all round. Lace the fabric over the card, keeping the lacing stitches well in from the edges so that they will not show when the box carcass is in position.

Place the carcass centrally on the covered platform base (laced surface uppermost) on a firm surface and pin securely into position. Stitch the carcass to the platform base, all round the lower edge of the carcass, using ladder stitch and a curved needle.

Lid:

Cut a piece of outer fabric to cover the card Y, allowing a margin of 30mm all round. Place the fabric on a firm surface, wrong side uppermost. Cut a piece of padding the same size as Y and position the padding centrally and then the piece of card Y on top. Lace the fabric over the card, keeping the lacing stitches well in from the edges.

An additional piece of card will be required if it is intended to embellish the lid with an embroidered panel. (See pages 10-14 for instructions as to how this can be done.)

Lid lining

Cut a piece of inner fabric to cover the card Z, allowing a margin of 20mm all round, and lace the fabric over the card. Position the lid lining card centrally on the covered lid, laced surfaces together, and stitch into place all round the edge of the lining card, using a curved needle.

2. "COLOUR THROUGH GOLD" ON LID OF A SMALL SQUARE BOX LID

The colours of the rayon threads used to create the "Colour through Gold" panel on the lid of this box were chosen to co-ordinate with the outer covering fabric, manufactured by Hi-Fashion Fabrics Inc., Design "NILE".

Materials

7" square of Congress Cloth
1 reel each of Madeira Rayon No. 30 in:

Mauve	1122
Yellow	1025
Tan	1174
Cerise	1183

1 reel of Madeira Gold metallic thread No. 12, col. 33
1 yard of gold ribbon 7mm wide
1 packet of mauve beads
1 packet of petite gold beads

Equipment

7" square wooden frame
No. 24 tapestry needle
Beading needle
Sharp embroidery scissors
Staples or drawing pins

Preparation

The finished "Colour through Gold" panel.

Stretch the Congress Cloth onto the frame using staples or drawing pins. If drawing pins are used, cover the heads with masking tape to avoid the threads catching on them.

Mark the starting point 3" down and 2" in from the left-hand side of the Congress Cloth.

Embroidery

Working from the full panel diagram, the coloured rayon threads are used in six thicknesses (use three threads through the needle, doubled) for the vertical stitches, and the gold metallic thread is used double throughout. For the border, reduce the rayon threads to two threads doubled.

Consult the charts and the photograph of the finished piece to ensure the stitches are placed in the correct positions and the right colours used.

Starting at the marked point (see 2.2) with the mauve thread, work the row of triangles at the top of the central square, which gives the straight edge.   Still using the mauve thread, work the first row of diamonds.   This is followed by a row of diamonds worked with both two mauve and two cerise threads doubled over.

The next row of diamonds is then worked in four tan threads doubled over and then another row in two tan threads and two yellow threads.   Carry on in this way until the coloured part of the central square is completed.

Using the gold metallic thread doubled, work the gold threads as shown on the charts - two rows, miss a row, and then two more rows.   The space is then filled with three beads - a gold, a mauve, another gold - use the tan thread doubled to attach the beads.

2.1 Chart for the central panel

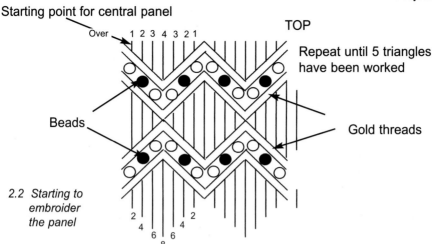

Starting point for central panel

Over   1 2 3 4 3 2 1

TOP

Repeat until 5 triangles have been worked

Beads

Gold threads

2.2 *Starting to embroider the panel*

A border is then worked around the embroidery with diagonal stitches over four threads using two tan threads doubled. Note that the corners overlap and the direction of stitches changes halfway along each side. Look carefully at the photograph to check these details - see 2.4.

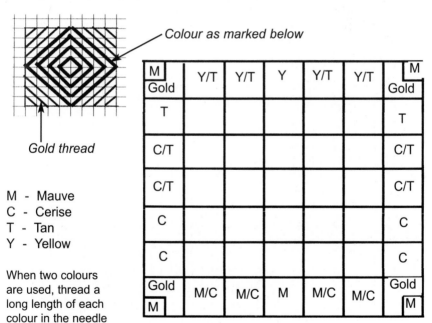

Colour as marked below

Gold thread

M - Mauve
C - Cerise
T - Tan
Y - Yellow

When two colours are used, thread a long length of each colour in the needle and double them over to give four thicknesses.

M Gold	Y/T	Y/T	Y	Y/T	Y/T	M Gold
T						T
C/T						C/T
C/T						C/T
C						C
C						C
Gold M	M/C	M/C	M	M/C	M/C	Gold M

2.3 *Chart for the outer border stitches*

The four central borders are worked in diagonal stitches to form diamonds. See the chart on the previous page to find the colours of the diamonds.

The four corners of the design are then worked.   First the small square is worked in mauve over four threads and then bordered on two sides with gold.   Using gold metallic thread, work diagonal stitches over four threads - note that each stitch points to the centre of the design.   The embroidery is now complete.

As shown in the photograph below, the "Colour through Gold" panel has been stitched onto a piece of the fabric used to line the box. It has been outlined with gold ribbon, which is stitched into place with petite gold beads. It was then laced over a piece of card cut so as to allow for an appropriate margin all round when positioned on the lid of the box.

The box lid is laced with the outer fabric and the embroidered panel positioned centrally and stitched into place using ladder stitch and a curved needle.   (See pages 10-14 for full instructions on embellishing lids.)

2.4   The completed box with the "Colour through Gold" panel on the lid.

3. BUTTERFLY & PANSY ON A SMALL SQUARE BOX LID

The fabric chosen for this small double-layer box, the internal measurements of which are approximately 4" x 4" x 2.5", is Pansies by Burgos for Marcus Bros. Textiles Inc. and the embroidery is long-and-short stitch shading, based on the colours in the fabric, surmounted by a stumpwork butterfly.

Materials
8" square of cotton fabric used for the box lining
8" square of cream cotton fabric
Small quantities of Pearsall's filoselle silk embroidery thread in:

Willow green	253 (palest)
" "	255
" "	256 (darkest)
Pink fawn	204
Navy blue	276
Maize gold	096
" "	097A
" "	099
Cream white	087
Pomegranate	282
Cornflower blue	249
" "	250
" "	251

2 x No. 28 cake wires
Circle (2" radius) of Vilene extra heavy interfacing
Reel of Gutermann sewing cotton to match the box lining fabric

Equipment
8" circular wooden embroidery frame
Fine embroidery needle
2" radius circle of card - mount board or similar
Sharp pencil
Sharp embroidery scissors
Fraycheck to seal edges (optional)

Preparation
Stretch the box lining fabric onto one of the frames - this will be the background fabric. Position the pansy design behind this fabric and lightly mark the design on the fabric in pencil. Stretch the cream cotton fabric onto the other frame - the butterfly wings will be worked on this fabric.

<u>Embroidery</u>

Split stitch around the flower petals in two strands of maize gold 097A.   The petals are worked in long and short stitch shading, making sure that the second and following rows go up in between the stitches of the first row so that the colours merge well.   Follow the colours marked on chart 3.3. Throughout the embroidery, keep referring to the photograph of the finished piece for the placing of the colours and the direction of the stitches.

<u>Back petals</u>

Outer row   097A
2nd row   096
Finish with 087

3.3 Colour directions for long & short stitch shading

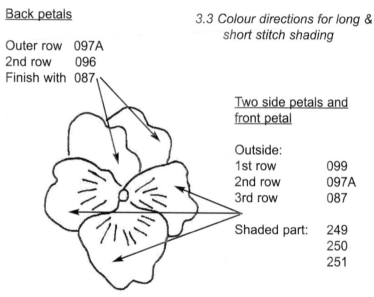

<u>Two side petals and front petal</u>

Outside:
1st row   099
2nd row   097A
3rd row   087

Shaded part: 249
                       250
                       251

The leaves are then worked, starting with the darkest green 256 outside, then adding 255 and finishing the leaves with 253.   Remember to keep the stitches at a sharp angle to the vein.

3.1 Small square double-layer box with embroidered pansy and stumpwork butterfly

3.2 Embroidery on the lid of the box on a hand-quilted background.

The pansy and its leaves are worked in long-and-short stitch shading.

3.4 Pansy background design showing the
head and body of the butterfly in position

Now, using the cream fabric on the second frame, mark the four wing shapes lightly with a pencil. Remember to leave sufficient space around each one to enable them to be cut out easily.

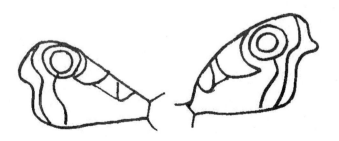

3.5 Two upper wing shapes for the butterfly

25

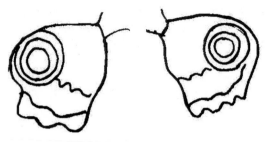

3.6 Two lower wing shapes for the butterfly

Lay the wire round the wing shape, couch it in place using a single strand of the navy thread 276.

Leaving the two wire ends loose, blanket stitch around the wire, again using 276, with small neat stitches close together. As you work the long and short stitches nearest to the wire, they will go over the wire and into the loops of the blanket stitches.

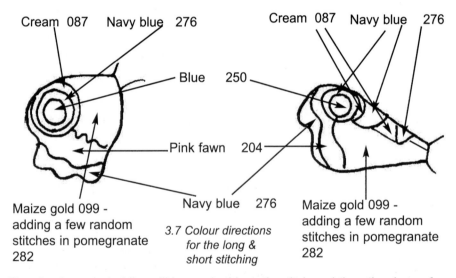

Cream 087   Navy blue 276   Cream 087   Navy blue   276

Blue   250

Pink fawn   204

Maize gold 099 - adding a few random stitches in pomegranate 282

Navy blue   276

Maize gold 099 - adding a few random stitches in pomegranate 282

3.7 Colour directions for the long & short stitching

The circular area in blue will be worked in satin stitch and then the rings of straight stitches in navy followed by cream will be added. The remainder of the wing will be worked in long and short stitch shading - refer to 3.7 for colour guidance. Work all four wings.

At this stage, you can go round the wing edges with fray check and allow this to dry completely - this is optional. The wings can now be carefully cut out as close to the stitches as you can get.

Lightly mark in pencil the background leaf shapes around the worked pansy. Cut out the circle of Vilene interfacing to go at the back of the work, saving a small scrap to cut out the head and body shape of the butterfly.

Pin the Vilene in place behind the pansy, ensuring that all the leaf markings are within the circle.   Back stitch through the interfacing and the background fabric all round the leaf shapes and add the veins.

   3.8 Head & body and feelers shapes for the butterfly

Carefully cut out the head and body shape and stitch in place, leaving the head free.   Bend a small piece of the cake wire to the shape shown in diagram 3.8 for the feelers.   The ends are bent over to form loops.

Lay a navy blue thread along the wire, secure in one of the loops and bind the wire with the thread along the length to the other loop.   The covered wire is then placed under the head and the head can then be stitched in place, thus securing the feelers.   Embroider the shape in satin stitch with the pink fawn silk thread.

The wire ends of the two lower wings can be put through the fabric by the side of the body and then the top wings' wires can be inserted above the lower wings.   Fold the ends of the wires over and secure by stitching to neaten.   Bend the wings to look natural.

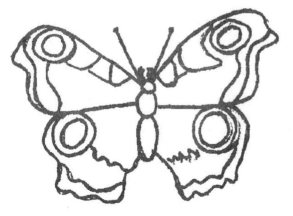

3.9 Shape of the finished butterfly

Put in a running stitch around the circle just outside the interfacing. Lay the card circle behind the interfacing and pull up the running stitching.   Lace across the circle to ensure there are no creases in the background.

This is now ready to be stitched onto the box lid using a curved needle.

4. NOTELET BOX

This rectangular box is made from pieces of card, covered with fabric and hand-sewn together, and is just the right size for the storage of notelets, stationery or correspondence and would also make a perfect gift. It could equally be used for recipes, needlework threads and equipment or just knick-knacks.

<u>Materials</u>

2mm greyboard
Two fat quarters of cotton fabric
   - one patterned fabric and one plain fabric
Strong thread for lacing
Sewing thread to match/tone with fabrics
Padding for lid

<u>Equipment</u>

Sharp pencil, set square and ruler
Cutting mat, sharp Stanley knife and metal safety ruler
Scissors, pins and sewing needles
Fine curved needle

The following diagram shows a bird's eye view of the finished carcass of the notelet box - the laced surfaces of card pieces are indicated by dotted lines.

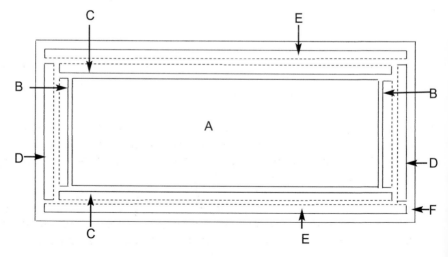

Bird's eye view of the notelet box on a platform base

Preparation

Identify the pieces of card as shown in the diagram on the opposite page.

Cut out the card, following the instructions given in the Basic Techniques section, to the following dimensions:

A	Inner base	225mm x 166mm	1
B	Inner sides	166mm x 40mm	2
C	Inner sides	230mm x 40mm	2
D	Outer sides	171mm x 40mm	2
E	Outer sides	235mm x 40mm	2

Method of construction

Allowing a margin of at least 20mm all round, cut pieces of lining fabric to cover pieces A, B (2) and C (2).   Lace each piece of fabric over the appropriate card.

Attach one covered side B, laced side outwards, to the covered base A, laced side downwards, using a matching sewing thread, ladder stitch with a curved needle, along the underside.

Stitch the second side B and the two sides C into place, in accordance with the bird's eye view diagram.   Stitch down the corners using ladder stitch with a curved needle.

Covering the outside of the box

Cut the fabric chosen for the outside of the box to cover the four side pieces D (2) and E (2), allowing 20mm turnings all round.   Lace each piece of fabric over the corresponding piece of card.

Position one covered side D in the correct place on the outside of the box, with the laced surface facing inwards, as shown in the bird's eye view diagram.   Stitch into position along all the edges, using ladder stitch with a curved needle.

Stitch the second side D into position and then add the two covered sides E, stitching these in the same way.   The two E pieces should exactly fit across C and the two Ds on either side - refer to the bird's eye view diagram 4.1 for the positions.

Platform Base

Cut a piece of card measuring 255mm x 195mm for the platform base F.

Cut a piece of outer fabric to cover the card piece F, allowing a margin of 30mm all round.

Lace the fabric over the card, keeping the lacing stitches well in from the edges so that they will not show when the box carcass is in position.

Place the carcass centrally on the covered platform base (laced surface upper-most) on a firm surface and pin securely into position. Using ladder stitch and a curved needle, stitch the box to the base around all sides.

Plain, padded lid

Cut a piece of card measuring 255mm x 195mm for the lid G and a piece of padding to the same dimensions.

Cut a piece of outer fabric to cover the card G, allowing a margin of 30mm all round.

Place the fabric on a firm surface, wrong side uppermost, position the padding centrally and then the piece of card G on top. Lace the fabric over the card, keeping the lacing stitches well in from the edges - this is to ensure that the lacing stitches will not show when the lining is in position. Bear in mind that a part of each of the mitred corners will show.

Lid lining

Cut a piece of card measuring 222mm x 163mm for the lid lining H - this can be cut from thin card if you prefer. Cut a piece of lining fabric to cover this card, allowing a margin of 20mm all round, and lace the fabric over the card.

Position the lid lining card centrally on the covered lid, laced surfaces together, and ladder stitch into place all round the edge of the lining card, using a curved needle. The covered lid should now sit on the box with its lining fitting neatly inside.

An embroidered panel can be stitched centrally onto the lid using ladder stitch with a curved needle.

5. NOTELET BOX LID WITH "COLOUR THROUGH GOLD"

The design for this embroidered panel has been "borrowed" from a patchwork idea.

Materials

10" x 8" rectangle of Congress Cloth
1 reel each of Madeira Rayon No. 40 in:

Pale yellow	1026
Tan	1173
Pale mauve	1311

1 reel each of Madeira Rayon No. 30 in:

Deep mauve	1112
Peacock	1185

1 reel of Madeira Gold metallic thread No. 12, col. 33
1 yard of gold ribbon 7mm wide
A piece of lining fabric 12" x 9"
Nymo 'D' gold beading thread
Small quantity of petite gold beads

Equipment

10" x 8" rectangular wooden frame
No. 24 tapestry needle
Beading needle
Sharp embroidery scissors
Staples or drawing pins

5.1   Finished notelet box with "Colour through Gold"

31

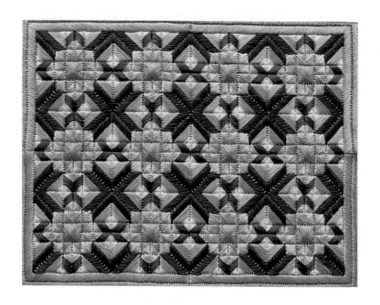

5.2   Completed "Colour through Gold" embroidered panel

Preparation

Stretch the Congress Cloth onto the frame using either staples or drawing pins. If drawing pins are used, cover the heads with masking tape to avoid the threads catching on them.

Embroidery

The embroidered area is approximately 4¾" x 6¼", so start the embroidery diagonally about 1¼" from the lower left-hand corner of this area.

Using three long lengths of the tan rayon, doubled over to give six thicknesses (to avoid having any ends up by the needle), work a Rhodes stitch over eight threads, marked on diagram 5.3 as A.   Then work the small triangles, marked B, with four diagonal stitches, still using the tan rayon threads.

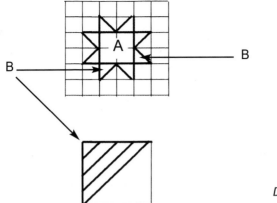

Diagram 5.3

The gold metallic thread is used doubled over to give two thicknesses and is used next to work the four corner squares in diagonal stitches, pointing towards the centre of the square - marked as C on diagram 5.4.

Diamonds of gold are then worked - these are marked D on diagrams 5.4 and 5.5.   Each quarter is worked with four stitches.

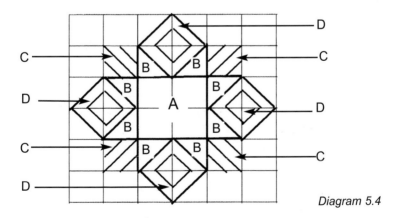

Diagram 5.4

The four corner areas in deep mauve - marked F in diagram 5.5 - are then worked with vertical and horizontal stitches over five threads.   The pale mauve diagonal stitches are then worked - note that the first stitch (nearest the deep mauve) uses holes already used.   Three diagonal stitches in pale yellow complete the corner squares.

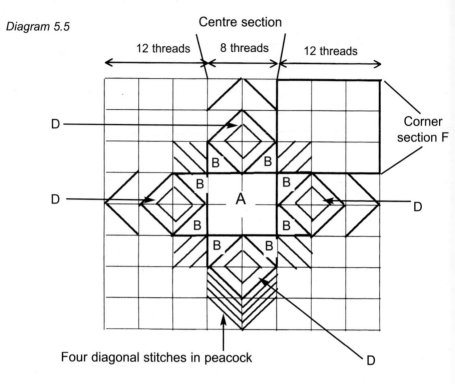

Diagram 5.5

The centre section already has the gold metallic diamond and then it has four diagonal stitches in peacock, followed by three in pale yellow.

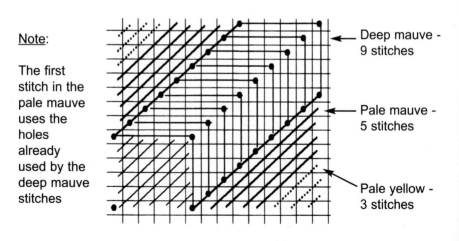

5.6 Corner section - F in diagram 5.5

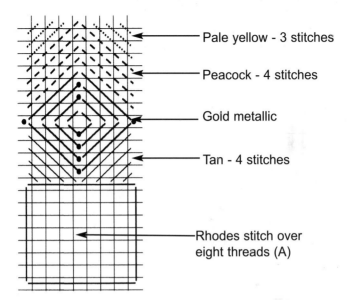

Pale yellow - 3 stitches

Peacock - 4 stitches

Gold metallic

Tan - 4 stitches

Rhodes stitch over
eight threads (A)

Diagram 5.7 - Centre Section

This square is repeated 11 more times as shown below in diagram 5.8.

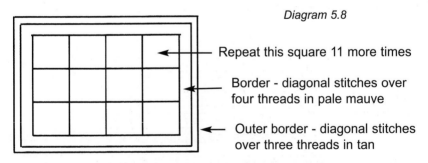

Diagram 5.8

Repeat this square 11 more times

Border - diagonal stitches over
four threads in pale mauve

Outer border - diagonal stitches
over three threads in tan

The whole area is then surrounded by diagonal stitches over four threads in pale mauve - note the change of direction half-way along each side. A further border of diagonal stitches in tan over three threads is worked to complete the panel.

Instructions for using ribbon and beads to mount the embroidery on the lining fabric prior to lacing over card and stitching onto the notelet box lid can be found on page 13.

6. NOTELET BOX WITH CASALGUIDI

This embroidery echoes the design of the fabric used for the lining of the box - make up the carcass of the notelet box as shown in project 4.

<u>Materials</u>
12" square 20 count Bellana or other suitable evenweave fabric

DMC Coton Perle 8:	Medium green	904
	Fawn	435
DMC Coton a Broder 16:	Mid green	702
	Red	666
DMC Coton Perle 5:	Green	229

1 reel of Madeira Gold metallic thread No. 12, col. 33
Piece of card 190mm x 130mm
Red fabric (used for box lining) 190mm x 130mm
Extra heavy interfacing measuring 190mm x 130mm
2 gold beads 4mm

6.1 The completed notelet box

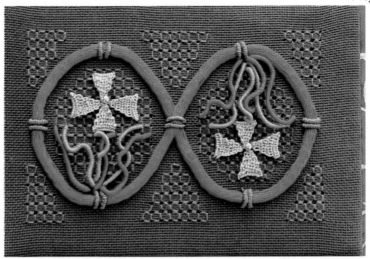

6.2 The finished Casalguidi embroidered panel

Equipment
10" circular wooden embroidery frame
Sharp embroidery scissors
Embroidery needle
No. 24 tapestry needle

Preparation
Stretch the evenweave fabric tightly into the frame.

Embroidery
Work a four-sided stitch background following the chart below and using
Coton Perle 8, medium green 904.

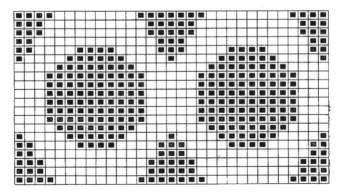

6.3   Four-sided stitch chart

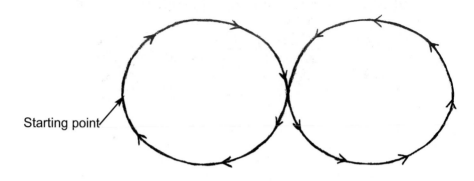

6.4   Positioning the raised stem bands

The raised red circles are worked as a padded, raised stem band, starting half way up the left side of the background.   The spaces between the four-sided stitch give the position for the band.

Begin by cutting 10 lengths of the fawn thread, each 24" long, which forms the padding for the raised bands.

Fold the threads in half and sew the looped end in the centre of the unworked space on the left-hand side - see starting point indicated in the diagram 6.4 above.   Start couching this in place with stitches about ¼" apart as shown in the 6.5 below.

6.5   Casalguidi - 1st stage

When the second circle has been completed, with another fawn thread, bind the end of the threads and cut them to meet the start of the band.

Cover the thread band with satin stitch using the embroidery needle and the fawn thread - see the photograph below 6.6.

6.6   Casalguidi - 2nd stage

Work a foundation of fawn stitches over the satin stitch, each stitch about ¼" apart - see photograph 6.7 below.

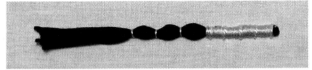

6.7 Casalguidi - 3rd stage

Work stem stitch in the red Coton a Broder taking one stitch over each bar of foundation stitches. Always work in the same direction. Use the tapestry needle for this and push each row over as it is worked to ensure the whole surface is covered - see photograph 6.8 below. Make sure you do not split the thread of the foundation bars.

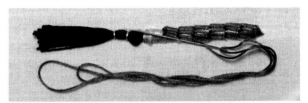

6.8 Casalguidi - 4th stage

The gold triangular shapes are worked in needlelace. Start by stitching two long stitches, each about ⅝" long on top of each other using a double gold metallic thread. Then a row of 10 blanket stitches are worked over the double thread. Keep working the rows into the loops of the previous row, decreasing by one stitch on each row to form a triangle. At the point of the triangle, go into the background fabric and fasten off. Work all four shapes in this way. Sew a gold bead in the centre.

Work the wrapped threads next - three red and three mid green in each circle. Eight threads are used as the core and then wrapped with a single thread of the Coton a Broder.

To complete the embroidery, work bullion knots (see the Stitch Glossary, page 134) in the Coton Perle 5 green 229 over the raised band in the position shown in the photograph of the finished piece 6.2.

The work is now ready to be stretched. Cut a piece of the red lining fabric and extra heavy interfacing to the size of the cut card top. Stitch the fabric and interfacing together. Stretch the embroidered panel over this and lace.

Follow the instructions given on page 30 for cutting the notelet box lid and lining. Cover the lid and lid lining cards with lining fabric. Stitch the embroidered panel onto the lid using ladder stitch and a curved needle.

7. NOTELET BOX WITH SHADED EMBROIDERY AND "COLOUR THROUGH GOLD"

The pansies are surrounded by "Colour through Gold" and the whole design is applied to the mauve background fabric with a border of gold ribbon. This finished design could be mounted and framed, put on a box lid or a bag or even used as a book cover. (This design on the lid of the notelet box originally appeared in Edition 18 of "Stitch with the Embroiderers' Guild" magazine - September/October 2002.)

<u>Materials</u>

10" x 8" rectangle of Congress Cloth
10" square of fine cream silk
10" square of cotton backing fabric
10" x 8" rectangle of mauve cotton fabric
1 reel each of Madeira Rayon No. 30 in:

Light green	1169
Mid green	1170
Dark green	1103
Pale lemon	1067
Mid yellow	1024
Tan	1173
Deep mauve	1112
Pinky mauve	1031

7.1   Finished notelet box

7.2   Shaded pansies embroidery with "Colour through Gold" surround

1 reel of Madeira Rayon No. 40 in: Medium mauve   1311

1 reel of Madeira Gold metallic thread No. 12, col. 33
1 yard of gold ribbon 7 mm wide
Small quantity of petite gold beads
Nymo 'D' gold beading thread

Equipment

8" circular wooden embroidery frame
10" x 8" rectangular wooden frame
Sharp embroidery scissors
Beading needle
Embroidery needle
No. 24 tapestry needle
Sharp pencil
Staples or drawing pins

Preparation

Place the design for the group of pansies and leaves (7.3 on page 43) under the backing cotton and mark the design with a sharp pencil onto the right side of the fabric.

Lay the silk over the cotton and check that you can see the design through it. If you cannot see the design, lightly mark it on to the silk by holding it up to a window or use a light box.

Stretch the silk and cotton fabrics together in the circular frame, so that the fabrics lie at the 'bottom' of the frame.   To achieve this, place the big ring onto the table, lay the two fabrics - with the silk uppermost - over it and put the smaller ring inside.

Stretch the Congress Cloth onto the rectangular frame using either staples or drawing pins.   If drawing pins are used, it is advisable to cover the heads with masking tape to avoid the threads catching on them.

Embroidery

When working the shading with the Madeira Rayon No. 30, only a single thread is used but, with the medium mauve thread, a double thread is used as the Madeira Rayon No. 40 is a slightly thinner rayon.

Outline the leaves and work the central vein in two strands of light green 1169 using back stitch. The leaves are then shaded using long and short stitch beginning with light green 1169 - this row goes over the back stitch edging - then using mid green 1170 and finishing with dark green 1103. Remember to keep your stitches at a sharp angle to the vein.

The stems are worked in straight stitches using light green 1169.

Using a double thread, back stitch around the petals of the larger central pansy with deep mauve 1112.   Start the shading of the back two petals with the same mauve thread using a single thread and going over the back-stitched edge.   Then using a double thread of the medium mauve 1311, work a second round.

Complete both of these petals with the pinky mauve 1031, again with only a single strand.

The next two petals are edged with the deep mauve, followed by a round of two threads of the medium mauve, then a round of the pale lemon and finally work a fan of stitches to complete the marking with the deep mauve.

The two little half-moon shapes which form the centre of the flower are worked in satin stitch with the pale lemon 1067 - see photograph 7.2.

7.3   Drawing for pansies and leaves

The front petal is outlined with long and short stitch in the pinky mauve 1031, followed by pale lemon 1067 and then a round of mixed deep mauve 1112 and medium mauve 1311.

The centre area is worked in the mid yellow 1024. To complete the flower, a single French knot is worked in the very centre in light green 1169.

The right-hand pansy is outlined with the pinky mauve 1031 and this thread is used to work the first round of each of the petals.   The back two petals were completed with the pale lemon 1067.

The next two petals and the front one are again worked with a pale lemon 1067 round, a pinky mauve 1031 round and finished with the deep mauve 1112.

The two little half-moon shapes at the centre are worked in satin stitch in the pale lemon 1067 and the flower is finished with a single French knot in light green 1169.

The left-hand pansy is outlined in back stitch using a double thread of mid yellow 1024.   The two back petals have a round of mid yellow 1024 and are finished with tan 1173.

The other three petals start with a round of pale lemon 1067, followed by a mid yellow round 1024, then a mixed round of mauves 1031 and 1311 and is finished with the deep mauve 1112.

"Colour through Gold" border

The rayon thread is worked using two threads in the needle, doubled over to give four thicknesses.   The metallic thread is used doubled over to give two thicknesses in the needle.   For all this work, use the No. 24 tapestry needle.

Place the circular frame centrally over the Congress Cloth stretched in the rectangular frame.   Pin the fabric to the Congress Cloth to hold it in place. The rice stitch surround can now be worked, following chart 7.4 (opposite) for the colours.

Starting with the rice stitch indicated by a star on the chart, these stitches are worked through both the fabric and the Congress Cloth.   (Check by looking carefully at the photograph 7.2 and chart 7.4 for the position of the first stitch.)

Each initial cross is worked over four threads and then the corners are crossed with the gold metallic thread, which is used double.   When two colours are mixed, a long thread of each colour is doubled to give four thicknesses in the needle.

The four corners are worked over 20 threads. Remember each cross-cornered cushion stitch is made up of four squares, each over 10 threads, all the stitches go into the centre of the finished square.   The under stitches are worked in deep mauve 1112.   Again the gold metallic thread is used for the overlaying stitches and these lie in the opposite direction to the deep mauve.

Between the four corners are Rhodes stitches, each worked over 8 threads and in the colours shown on the chart.

Finally, a rice stitch border is worked around the entire design - the initial cross in deep mauve and corners crossed with gold metallic thread.

Surround the flowers and leaves with a zig-zag back stitch worked in the pale lemon 1067.

See page 13 for instructions on mounting the embroidery onto the background fabric of the lid using ribbon and beads.

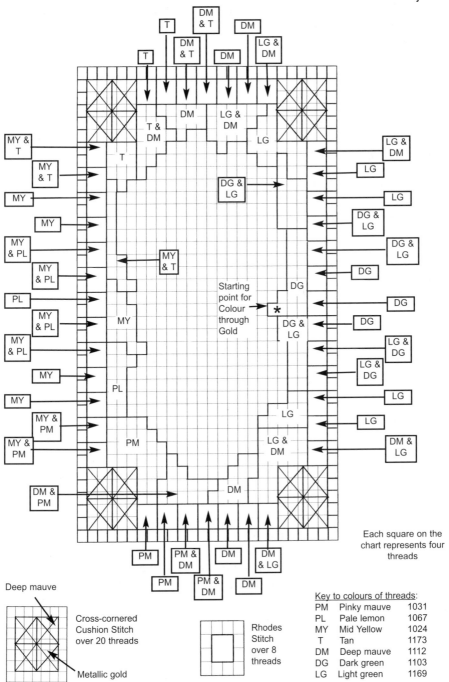

Each square on the chart represents four threads

Deep mauve

Cross-cornered
Cushion Stitch
over 20 threads

Metallic gold

Rhodes
Stitch
over 8
threads

Key to colours of threads:

PM	Pinky mauve	1031
PL	Pale lemon	1067
MY	Mid Yellow	1024
T	Tan	1173
DM	Deep mauve	1112
DG	Dark green	1103
LG	Light green	1169

7.4 Chart for the "Colour through Gold" surround for the shaded pansies

45

8. NOTELET BOX WITH DIVIDED LID

This rectangular box is similar to the notelet box featured on page 28 but a divided and hinged lid has been added.

Materials

2mm greyboard
½ metre of patterned fabric for outer covering
½ metre of plain fabric for the lining
Strong thread for lacing
Sewing thread to match/tone with fabrics

Equipment

Sharp pencil, set square and ruler
Cutting mat, sharp knife and metal safety ruler
Scissors, pins and sewing needles
Fine curved needle

Diagram 8.1 below shows a bird's eye view of the internal notelet box; the laced surfaces of the card pieces are indicated by dotted lines.

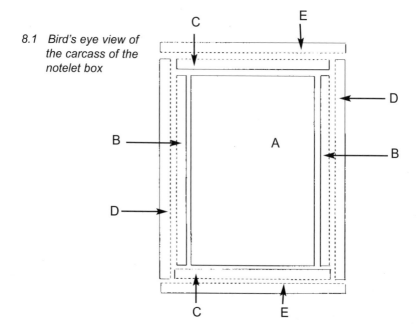

8.1 *Bird's eye view of the carcass of the notelet box*

Method of construction

Cut out the card, following the instructions given on page 5, to the following dimensions:

A	Inner base	225mm x 166mm	1
B	Inner sides	225mm x 35mm	2
C	Inner sides	172mm x 35mm	2
D	Outer sides	231mm x 35mm	2
E	Outer sides	178mm x 35mm	2

Cut the fabric chosen for the lining of the box to cover card pieces A, B (2) and C (2), allowing a margin of at least 20mm all round. Lace each piece of fabric over the appropriate card.

Attach one covered side B, laced side outwards, to the covered base A, laced side downwards, using a matching sewing thread, ladder stitch, and a curved needle, along the underside.

Stitch the second side B and the two sides C into place, in accordance with the bird's eye view diagram. Stitch down the corners using ladder stitch with a curved needle.

Covering the outside of the box

Cut the fabric chosen for the outside of the box to cover the four side pieces D (2) and E (2), allowing 20mm turnings all round. Lace each piece of fabric over the corresponding piece of card.

Position one covered side D in the correct place on the outside of the box, with the laced surface facing inwards, as shown in the bird's eye view diagram 8.1. Stitch into position along all the edges, using ladder stitch and a curved needle.

Stitch the second side D into position and then add the two covered sides E, stitching these in the same way.

Hinges

Cut sufficient lining fabric which, when folded, stitched and the seams pressed open, will form a double piece of fabric measuring 170mm x 60mm. Make a second hinge in the same way. Stitch the hinges to the underside of the base, leaving 30mm protruding on each side.

8.2   Stitching hinges to the underside of the base of the notelet box

<u>Platform Base</u>

Cut a piece of card measuring 261mm x 206mm for the platform base.   Cut a piece of outer fabric to cover the platform base, allowing a margin of 30mm all round.   Lace the fabric over the card, keeping the lacing stitches well in from the edges so that they will not show when the box carcass is in position.

Place the carcass centrally on the covered platform base (laced surface uppermost) on a firm surface and pin securely into position.   Using ladder stitch with a curved needle, stitch the box to the base around all sides, stitching through the hinges and along the front and back.

<u>Divided lid:</u>

Cut out the following pieces of card and the appropriate fabric for each, allowing a margin of 20mm all round, and lace the fabric over the card.

F	Lining sides	93mm x 39mm	4
G	Lining backs	239mm x 39mm	2
H	Lining tops	245mm x 93mm	2
I	Outer sides	97mm x 43mm	4
J	Outer backs	245mm x 43mm	2
K	Outer tops	251mm x 97mm	2

Assemble the two lids - using a curved needle with ladder stitch.   Sew the linings together first, as shown in the diagram 8.3.

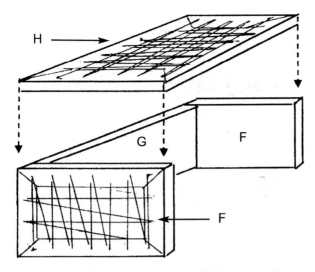

8.3   Stitching the pieces of the lid lining together

Position one lid on the box, fold the hinge upwards and sew the hinge to the inner back as closely and as low as possible.   Repeat with the second lid on the opposite side.

Insert the covered outer back pieces J and stitch into position along the two sides and the top of each.   The lower edge, alongside the platform base, remains unstitched.

Stitch the lid tops into position, using ladder stitch with a curved needle.

8.4   Finished divided-top notelet box

49

9.   DIVIDED-TOP BOX WITH STUMPWORK DRAGONFLIES

Needless to say, the design for the divided lid of this notelets box was totally inspired by the fabric used for the outside of the box.   The realistic dragonflies are worked in stumpwork techniques, using cake wires to make the wings three-dimensional.

Materials

2 x 15" square of box lining fabric
Vilene extra heavy interfacing - 2 pieces the size of the lid cards

Pearsall's filoselle silk embroidery thread:

1 skein each of:	Sage green	189
	" "	191
	" "	193
	Moonlight	316
	Silver grey	144
	China blue	209
	" "	210
	Orange yellow	148
	" "	153
	" "	155
	Maize gold	099

Fine, silver metallic thread
10" square of crystal chiffon
10" square of white cotton backing
16 Peacock blue 9mm bugle beads
6 oval beads (for the dragonfly body)
Silver seed beads
Tan seed beads (for the bulrush)
4 gold seed beads   )
4 mauve seed beads   )   for eyes
Nymo D beading thread
2 white cake wires No. 28

Equipment

12" and 8" circular wooden embroidery frames
Sharp embroidery scissors
Fine embroidery needle
Beading needle

Preparation

Stretch the first piece of lining fabric into the 12" embroidery frame.   Tack around the lid card to define the area in which the embroidery will be worked.

Trace the design (9.2) and place the tracing over the design area and tack through both the paper and fabric.   Tear away the tracing paper.

First Embroidery - waterlily and dragonfly

All the shading is worked in a single thread of the silk.   Outline each petal using split stitch and two strands of the Pale orange yellow silk 148.   Start shading from the outside of each petal using Orange yellow 148, continue with Orange yellow 153 and complete with Orange yellow 155.   Satin stitch the petal overlap using Orange yellow 155.   Work the flower centre with long-armed French knots in Moonlight 316 and then add the silver seed beads.

Work the water starting with two rows of stem stitch in Moonlight 316, followed by a row of chain stitch in Silver grey 144, two rows in China blue 209 and then a single row in China blue 210.

Outline the leaf in split stitch using two strands of the palest Sage green 189 and use this thread for starting the shading on the outside edge.   Continue with Sage green 191 and finally complete the leaf using Sage green 193.

9.1   Waterlily in shading and stumpwork

51

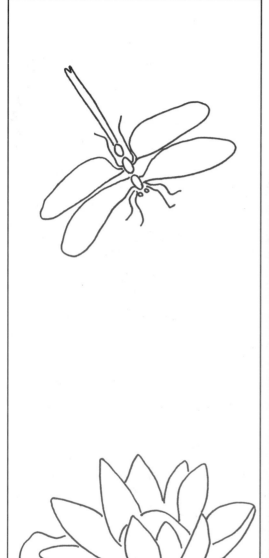

9.2   Pattern for waterlily and dragonfly design - enlarge to the required size.

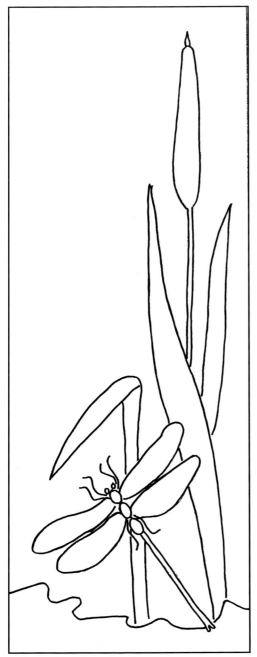

9.3   Pattern for dragonfly and bulrush design - enlarge to the required size.

9.4   Stumpwork wings & beaded body for the Dragonfly

Using the small embroidery ring, stretch the crystal chiffon over the cotton backing.   Using the template for the dragonfly wings, bend the wire and couch in place.   Using a single strand of Moonlight 316, blanket stitch over the wire.   The vein markings are then worked in back stitch using the silver metallic thread.   Cut out carefully, using really sharp scissors.

All the beads are stitched onto the fabric with the Nymo D thread and a beading needle.

Start working the tail with three silver beads, followed by two bugle beads, 1 silver seed bead, two bugle beads, a silver seed bead, two bugle beads, 1 silver seed bead and two bugle beads.   The first oval bead is then added.

Put the two wires of the first set of wings, one each side of the top of the oval bead, through the fabric.   The second oval bead is then stitched over the centre of the wings.   The second pair of wings is added with the third oval bead.

The eyes are then added, a mauve bead over a gold one.

Finally the silver thread is used to work the legs with straight stitches.

<u>Second embroidery - dragonfly and bulrush</u>

Stretch the fabric and apply the design as before. The water is embroidered, as for the first side, and the three leaves are stitched, starting at the top point with the palest green. The stem is worked in rows of stem stitch, starting with two rows of the palest green on the left side, then a single row of 191 and finishing with a single row of 193.

The bulrush is embroidered with French knots in maize gold 099 and the tan beads. At the top is a triangle of five straight stitches in 099.

The dragonfly can now be worked as before.

<u>Finishing the lid</u>

Cut two pieces of interfacing to the size of the lid card and place behind each embroidery. Stretch the fabric over the cards, lacing the long sides first. Stitch into position on the lid tops.

9.5   Divided top notelet box with shading and stumpwork

10. NOTELET BOX WITH EXTRA ENDS

Extra boxes have been added on either side of a notelet box to create a three-compartment box for the storage of stationery items.   Three lids give great opportunity for embellishment, either by way of embroidery and/or the use of very special fabrics.   Hi-Fashion Fabrics Inc. - Luxor-M1 fabric has been used for the outer covering of this box.

Materials

2mm greyboard
Thin card for lid linings (cereal card will be fine)
$^1/2$ metre of patterned fabric for outer covering
$^1/2$ metre of plain fabric for the lining
Strong thread for lacing
Sewing thread to match/tone with fabrics
Ribbon for stays
Padding for lids, if required

Equipment

Pencil, ruler and set square
Cutting mat, sharp knife and metal safety ruler
Scissors, pins and sewing needles
Small, fine, curved needle

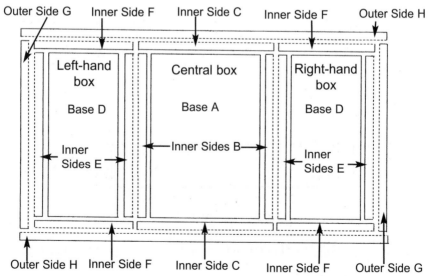

10. 1 Bird's eye view of the carcass of the stationery box

Method of construction

For the central box:

Cut out the card, according the instructions given on page 5, to the following dimensions:

A	Base	225mm x 166mm	1
B	Inner sides	225mm x 40mm	2
C	Inner sides	172mm x 40mm	2

Repeat the process for the left- and right-hand boxes, using the following dimensions:

D	Base	225mm x 87mm	2
E	Inner sides	225mm x 40mm	4
F	Inner sides	93mm x 40mm	4

Allowing a margin of at least 20mm all round, cut pieces of lining fabric to cover all the above pieces and lace the fabric over the appropriate card.

Assemble the three boxes, in accordance with the bird's eye view diagram 10.1, using ladder stitch with a curved needle.

Hinges

Each of the lids will be hinged, as shown in photographs 10.4 and 10.5, and these are created by folding 100mm-wide strips of fabric in half (right sides inside) and seaming across the ends so as to make the hinges 15mm shorter than the edge being hinged.   Trim the seams before turning the hinge inside out and pressing.

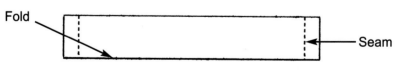

10.2   Creating a hinge

Fold each hinge over the relevant side of each box and tack into place on the laced surface, leaving 30mm to extend upwards for stitching between the lid and lining - see diagram 10.3.

Stays

Measure six 160mm lengths of ½" ribbon and pin to the laced surfaces of the boxes, in accordance with diagram 10.3 below. See the photographs on the opposite page and the diagram and instructions on page 108 for more advice about the angle and placing of stays.

Each of the stays should be positioned at the same distance from the back of the boxes, so that the lids will lie back at an even angle.

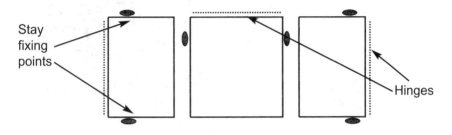

Stay fixing points

Hinges

10.3   Positioning the hinges and stays

Stitch the left- and right-hand boxes on either side of the central box, using ladder stitch and a curved needle. Ensure that the needle passes through the ribbons on the central box, so that these are firmly stitched in place.

Cut the following pieces of 2mm greyboard for the outer sides and lace with outer-covering fabric (allowing a margin of 20mm all round):

G	Outer sides	232mm x 40mm	2
H	Front and back	371mm x 40mm	2
I	Outer base	371mm x 238mm	1

Stitch sides G into place on the hinged edges of the side boxes, making sure the needle passes through the hinges, so that these are firmly stitched in place.   Stitch the pieces H to the front and back so that they lie across the three boxes and the two outer sides G, stitching through the ribbon stays at the same time.   Stitch the base I to the underside.

Lids

Cut the following pieces of 2mm greyboard for the central lid and the lids for the two outer boxes:

Central lid	244mm x 171mm	1
Outer lids	244mm x 102mm	2

and for the lid linings, cut from thin card:

Centre lid	222mm x 163mm	1
Outer lids	222mm x 84mm	2

Allowing a margin of 20mm all round, cut outer fabric and lining fabric and lace this over the appropriate cards, padding the lids if required.

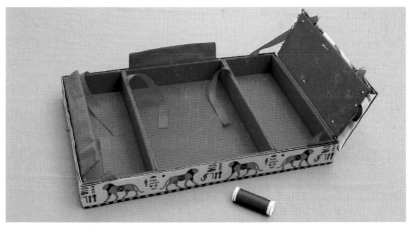

10.4   Carcass with hinges, stays and one lid pinned in position

Position and stitch each of the lids into place, following the instructions given on page 15 for hinging a lid.   Start with the lids of the outer boxes, stitching the central box lid into position last.

10.5   Notelet box with extra ends and an Egyptian theme

11. EGYPTIAN GODDESS ON STATIONERY BOX

The head of this Egyptian Goddess has been worked on silk noile with the headband in chain stitch, the comb in chain stitch outlined with stem stitch and then fully beaded.   The features are in long and short stitch, as is her hair and blouse.   The necklace and armbands are made of beads.

Materials

12" square of background fabric - natural colour
Indian rayon thread in: black, flesh colour, pale turquoise, dark turquoise,
        tan, cream and a very small amount of red for the lips
1 reel of Madeira gold metallic thread, No. 12, colour 33
A short length of white sewing thread for the socket of the eye
Seed beads - gold, bronze, turquoise, dark brown, yellow and fawn
1 blue seed bead (for the eye)
Nymo D Gold beading thread   9 mm bugle beads - peacock
2mm greyboard - 244mm x 171mm   Box lining fabric to cover the card
A piece of extra-heavy interfacing 9" x 6"

Equipment

10" circular wooden embroidery frame   Beading needle
Embroidery needle   Sharp pencil
Tracing paper   Sharp scissors
Usual sewing equipment

Preparation

Stretch the background fabric tightly into the circular frame.   Trace the outline of the Egyptian Goddess, diagram 11.1, using the sharp pencil and place this tracing on the top of the fabric.   With a running stitch, go round the design lines and then carefully tear the paper away.

Embroidery

All the long and short stitch in the design, with the exception of the hair, is worked in one strand of the rayon thread.   For the hair, as a less smooth surface is required, work with two threads and, for this design, the metallic gold thread is used double.

Using long and short stitch and the pale turquoise thread, work the blouse top, changing the direction of the stitches to denote the armhole.   The

11.1   Template for Egyptian Goddess embroidery

straps are worked in chain stitch, a row of dark turquoise each side and filled
with rows of tan.   Her dress has rows of chain stitch around the top: two
rows of dark turquoise and then single rows of pale turquoise, gold, dark
turquoise, gold, pale turquoise and finish with a double row of dark turquoise.
The remainder is worked in diagonal rows of chain stitch - refer to the
photograph 11.3 on page 63 for the colours.

Her arms and neck are worked in long and short stitch, ensuring that the directions of the stitches follow the contours of the face features and ear, leaving spaces for the eye and mouth.   Work the lips in red satin stitch and the eye socket in white, outlining the eye and adding the eyebrow in black thread.   Use a single blue bead for the iris.   Two small black stitches define the nostrils and a single bronze bead is used as an earring.

Work the main part of the hair in long and short stitch and use satin stitch for the four ringlets.

Her head-band is worked in a double row of pale turquoise chain stitch, with a row of gold on either side.

For her arm bands, use beads, stitched on following the sequence shown in diagram 11.2 below.

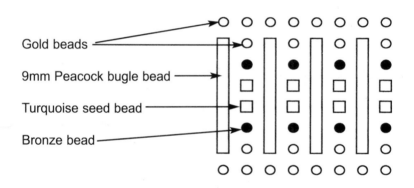

11.2   *Beading sequence for the arm bands*

For the necklace, starting at the lower edge, each row of beads is threaded on as one long string to the required length and caught down in two or three places.

Row 1 has alternate gold and bronze beads to the required length
　　　　Row 2 - 1 gold, 1 bronze, 2 turquoise and 1 bronze repeated.
　　　　Row 3 as Row 1
　　　　Row 4 - all in gold
　　　　Row 5 - as row 2
　　　　Row 6 - as Row 1

Continue adding rows in gold beads until the area is filled.

11.3   Embroidered Egyptian Goddess head for central lid of stationery box

The comb head-dress is outlined in a row of gold chain stitch.   The shaft of
the feather has an additional row of gold stem stitch outside the chain stitch.
The feather is filled with alternate rows of beads: 1 gold, 1 bronze, 1 bugle,
   bronze and 1 gold, followed by 9 seed beads - gold and bronze used
alternately.

The foreground is filled with tan French knots and dark brown, yellow and fawn seed beads randomly spaced.

Next cut out a piece of extra-heavy interfacing to the outline shape of the design and place this centrally beneath the embroidery. Using small back stitches, zig zag all around the design and between the arms and body on the unstitched background, using a single gold metallic thread.

Cut all round the design, leaving a margin of 20mm (¾") outside the interfacing. Turn the fabric over to the wrong side and herring-bone in place; it will be necessary to snip into the turnings round the curved edges.

Place the embroidery centrally onto the lining fabric and attached using small bronze beads at regular intervals. Next, lace the fabric over the piece of greyboard and then, using ladder stitch with a curved needle, stitch into position on the already prepared lid.

11.4   Stationery box with Egyptian Goddess embroidered on the central lid

12. NAPKIN BOX

This box has been designed to contain a supply of paper napkins, size 150mm x 150mm (6" x 6"), and could be made up in appropriate fabrics for seasonal celebrations.

Materials

2mm greyboard
¼ metre (or a fat quarter) of patterned fabric for outer covering
¼ metre (or a fat quarter) of plain fabric for the lining
Strong thread for lacing
Sewing thread to match/tone with fabrics
Padding for the lid (optional)

Equipment

Pencil, ruler and set square
Cutting mat, sharp knife and metal safety ruler
Scissors, pins and sewing needles
Small, fine curved needle

12.1 Napkin box

Preparation

Rule up the greyboard and cut out to the following dimensions - refer to page 5 for advice on this procedure.

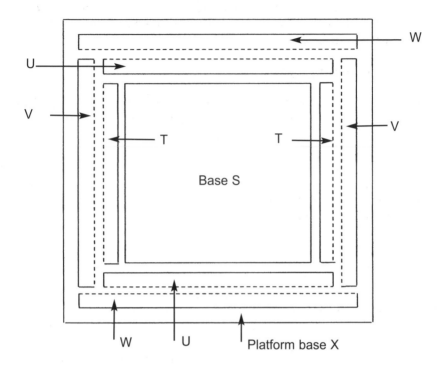

*12.2   Bird's eye view of the carcass of the napkin box; the laced
surfaces of the card pieces are indicated by dotted lines*

S	Inside base	170mm x 170mm	1
T	Inner sides	170mm x 60mm	2
U	Inner sides	176mm x 60mm	2
V	Outer sides	176mm x 60mm	2
W	Outer sides	182mm x 60mm	2
X	Platform base	197mm x 197mm	1
Y	Lid	197mm x 197mm	1
Z	Lid lining	166mm x 166mm	1

<u>Method of construction</u>

Cut lining fabric for each of the card pieces S, T (2) and U (2), allowing a
margin of 20mm all round, and lace the fabric over the appropriate card.

Attach one covered side T, laced side outwards, at right angles to the
covered base S, laced side downwards, stitching along the underside.   Use
a matching sewing thread and ladder stitch with a curved needle.

Stitch the second side T and the two sides U into place, in accordance with the bird's eye view diagram 12.1. Stitch down the corners using ladder stitch with a curved needle.

Covering the outside of the box

Allowing 20mm turnings all round, cut the fabric chosen for the outside of the box to cover the four side pieces V (2) and W (2), . Lace each piece of fabric over the corresponding piece of card.

Position one covered side V in the correct place on the outside of the box, with the laced surface facing inwards, as shown in the bird's eye view diagram 12.1. Stitch into position along all the edges, using ladder stitch with a curved needle. Stitch the second side V into position and then add the two covered sides W, stitching these in the same way.

Platform Base:

Cut a piece of outer fabric to cover the card X, allowing a margin of 30mm all round. Lace the fabric over the card, keeping the lacing stitches well in from the edges so that they will not show when the box carcass is in position.

Place the carcass centrally on the covered platform base (laced surface uppermost) on a firm surface and pin securely into position. Using ladder stitch and a curved needle, stitch the carcass to the platform base, all round the lower edge of the carcass,

Plain padded lid

Cut a piece of outer fabric to cover the card Y, allowing a margin of 30mm all round. Place the fabric on a firm surface, wrong side uppermost, position the padding centrally and then the piece of card Y on top.

Lace the fabric over the card, keeping the lacing stitches well in from the edges - this is to ensure that the lacing stitches will not show when the lid lining is in position.

Lid lining

Allowing a margin of 20mm all round, cut a piece of lining fabric to cover the card Z, and lace the fabric over the card. Position the lining card centrally on the covered lid, laced surfaces together, and stitch into place all round the edge of the lining card, using ladder stitch with a curved needle.

13. NAPKIN BOX WITH BARGELLO INSET PANEL IN THE LID

The Bargello (sometimes called Florentine) design shown on the top of the napkin box in the photograph opposite (13.2), was worked on Congress Cloth using two strands of Anchor stranded cotton.

Materials
6" square of Congress Cloth
8 skeins of Anchor stranded cotton:

         5 colours ranging from cream through to pink
         3 shades of green ranging from pale to dark

Equipment
6" square wooden embroidery frame
Tapestry needle no. 24
Embroidery scissors
Staples or drawing pins

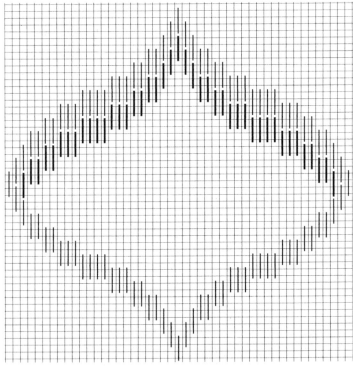

13.1   Chart for establishing the first stitches in the Bargello design

Preparation

Stretch the Congress Cloth onto the embroidery frame, using either staples or drawing pins - if using the latter, cover with masking tape to avoid the threads catching on them.

Embroidery

Mark the centre of the Congress Cloth and, using two strands of the palest cream, bring the needle up at a point approximately 30mm above the centre. Work straight vertical stitches over four threads of the cloth following the pomegranate design shown in the chart 13.1 opposite. Once the first round of stitches has been established, the next colour of the stranded cotton is taken and another row worked immediately below the first.

Use the photograph of the finished design 13.2 to follow the colour changes and the arrangement of the stitches.

See pages 10 and 11 for instructions as to how to inset the embroidered panel into the padded lid.

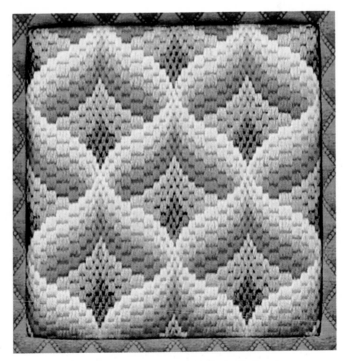

13.2 Lid of napkin box with Bargello inset

14. NAPKIN BOX WITH BEADED LID

The decoration on this box lid was adapted directly from the fabric chosen for the outer covering but the design could also be used on a plainer fabric. The beading on the box lid in the photograph required the following:

Materials

No. 11 seed beads in three co-ordinating colours
9mm bugle beads in the same three colours
Larger beads for the centres
Nymo D beading thread
1 reel of Madeira gold metallic thread No. 12, colour 33
Circles of extra heavy interfacing
Fabric as used for the lining of the box

Equipment

8" circular wooden embroidery frame
Beading needle
Embroidery and fabric-cutting scissors

Embroidery

The large circle was worked on a small ring frame with the fawn fabric stretched into it and a circle of extra heavy interfacing put underneath. The beading was then worked within a framework of gold stitching - the design for this was suggested by the fabric.

A smaller circle of interfacing was covered in the same fabric and placed centrally on the circle and beaded. The fabric was then removed from the frame and a circle of running stitches was worked ½" outside the interfacing and pulled up so that the remaining circular shape could be attached to the background fabric, which was stretched into the 8" frame. This was also backed by an interfacing circle.

A double strand of gold thread was couched around the attached circle and followed by two more couched thread rounds. The smaller and medium circles were then worked on the background fabric.

The background was spot beaded using the design on the fabric to suggest their position. This was then stretched over a circle of card cut to a suitable size and attached to the lid using a curved needle.

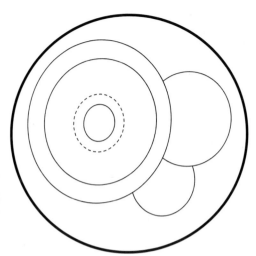

14.1 Suggested design for beaded embroidery on the lid of napkin box (enlarge and amend as required)

14.2 Fabric used for the outer covering and the basis for the beading design on the lid

14.3 Final design for the beading on the napkin box

15. NAPKIN BOX WITH DIVIDED LID

The distinctive feature of this box is the division of the lid as the box is opened.   This box would be the right size for the storage of paper napkins but it would also make an attractive keepsakes box.   Accurate cutting of the fabrics to allow patterns to be matched across the top and sides requires more fabric than is suggested in the list.

Materials

2mm greyboard
½ metre of patterned cotton fabric for outer covering
½ metre of plain or contrasting cotton fabric for the lining
Strong thread for lacing
Sewing thread to match/tone with fabrics

Equipment

Sharp pencil, ruler and set square
Cutting mat, sharp knife and metal safety ruler
Scissors, pins and sewing needles
Fine curved needle

Method of construction

Cut out greyboard to the following dimensions - see page 5 for advice on this procedure:

Inner box

A	Inside Base	170mm x 170mm	1
B	Inner Sides	170mm x 60mm	2
C	Inner Sides	176mm x 60mm	2
D	Outer Sides	176mm x 60mm	2
E	Outer Sides	182mm x 60mm	2

Divided lid tops

F	Inner Sides	95mm x 64mm	4
G	Inner Backs	184mm x 64mm	2
H	Inner Tops	190mm x 95mm	2
I	Outer Sides	98mm x 67mm	4
J	Outer Backs	190mm x 67mm	2
K	Outer Tops	196mm x 98mm	2
L	Platform Base	210mm x 210mm	1

Allowing a margin of 20mm all round, cut fabric to cover each of the following pieces of card and lace the fabric over the appropriate card.

A	Inside base	1	)	to be laced
B	Inner sides	2	)	with lining
C	Inner sides	2	)	fabric
D	Outer sides	2	)	to be laced
E	Outer sides	2	)	with outer fabric

Attach one covered side B, laced side outwards, to the covered base A, laced side downwards, using a matching sewing thread, ladder stitch with a curved needle, along the underside.

Stitch the second side B and the two sides C into place, in accordance with the bird's eye view diagram. Stitch down the corners using ladder stitch with a curved needle.

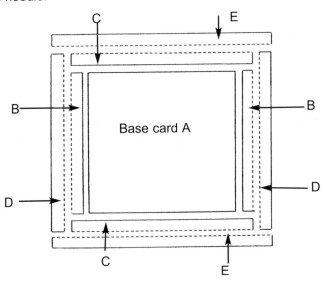

15.1   *Bird's eye view of the basic carcass of the divided top box*
- the laced surfaces are indicated by dotted lines

Covering the outside of the box

Cut the fabric chosen for the outside of the box to cover the four side pieces D (2) and E (2), allowing 20mm turnings all round. Lace each piece of fabric over the corresponding piece of card. Position one covered side D in the correct place on the outside of the box, with the laced surface facing inwards, as shown in the bird's eye view diagram 15.1.

Stitch into position along all the edges, using ladder stitch and a curved needle.　Stitch the second side D into position and then add the two covered sides E, stitching these in the same way.

<u>Hinges</u>

Cut sufficient fabric which, when folded, stitched and the seams pressed open, will form a double piece of fabric measuring 170mm x 60mm.　Make a second hinge in the same way.　Stitch the hinges to the underside of the base, leaving 30mm protruding on each side.

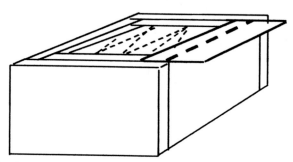

15.2　Stitching a hinge to one edge of the underside of the base

<u>Platform Base</u>

Cut a piece of outer fabric to cover the card L, allowing a margin of 30mm all round.　Lace the fabric over the card, keeping the lacing stitches well in from the edges so that they will not show when the carcass is in position.

Place the carcass centrally on the covered platform base (laced surface uppermost) on a firm surface and pin securely into position.　Using ladder stitch with a curved needle, stitch the box to the base around all sides, stitching through the hinges and along the front and back.

<u>Divided lid</u>

Allowing a margin of 20mm all round, cut the appropriate fabric for each of the following pieces of card, and lace the fabric over the card.

```
F  Inner Sides  4     ) to be laced
G  Inner Backs  2     ) with lining
H  Inner Tops   2     ) fabric
                          I  Outer Sides  2     ) to be laced
                          J  Outer Backs  2     ) with outer
                          K  Outer Tops   2     ) fabric
```

Assemble the two lids - using a curved needle with ladder stitch. Sew the linings together first, as shown in diagram15.3 below, and then add the outer sides I (4) and the tops K (2).

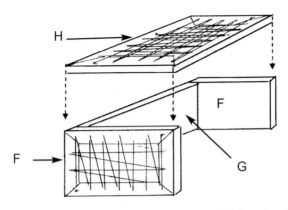

H ———→

F

F ———→

G

15.3 Stitching the pieces of the lid linings together

Position one lid on the box, fold the hinge upwards and sew the hinge to the inner back G of the lid as closely and as low as possible.   Repeat with the second lid on the opposite side.

Insert the covered outer back pieces J and stitch into position along the two sides and the top of each. The lower edge, adjacent to the platform base, remains unstitched.   Stitch the lid tops into position, using ladder stitch with a curved needle.

15.4   Finished divided-lid napkin box

16. NAPKIN BOX WITH MACHINE-EMBROIDERED POPPIES AND DAISIES ON DIVIDED LID

Machine embroidery is used for the decoration of this divided box but of course the same design could be hand embroidered. It also has beads, straight stitches and French knots as embellishment.

Materials

2 x 12" squares of lining fabric
2 pieces of extra heavy interfacing the size of the box lids
1 reel each of:Gutermann 100% Polyester sewing thread:

- Darkest red	368	gradually	
	46	getting	
	156	paler	
- Palest orange	285	for the poppy	
- White		for the daisies	
- Blue	213	and	
	143	cornflowers	
- Green	931	be used	
	913	for	
- Corn	979	both lids	

1 reel to match the background fabric

Small amount of white shiny Indian rayon thread (if available)
Small amount of yellow, dark blue, pale green and black stranded cotton for French knots and bullion knots
Small amount of black, yellow, gold and blue seed beads
Cut 2mm greyboard for lid tops - K from Project 15

Equipment

10" circular wooden embroidery frame
Embroidery needle
Beading needle
Sharp embroidery scissors

Sharp pencil
Tracing paper
Sewing machine

Preparation

Stretch one piece of the lining fabric tightly into the frame, keeping the fabric in the 'well' of the frame - place the larger ring on the table, add the fabric and stretch with the smaller ring.

16.1   Design for Poppy
lid top

16.2   Design for Daisy
lid top

N.B.   These designs have been reduced in scale in order to fit them onto the page.   Enlarge each design on a photocopier to increase the size to fit on the tops of the divided lids.   The pieces of greyboard K measure 196mm x 98mm - see the instructions for making the divided top box - project 15 - on page 72.

Embroidery

Poppies

Trace the poppy design 16.1 and enlarge to fit lid top K. Place the tracing under the fabric and, with a pencil, mark it onto the fabric. Drop the lower feed teeth of the machine and remove the presser foot.

Outline the flower petals and the two buds in the darkest red 368 and use this to start the shading beginning on the outside edge and going out over the outline stitching.

Carry on the shading to complete the petals using 46, 156 and finally 285. (Do not stitch the flower centre)

Next outline the sepals , leaves and stems of the flowers in the brighter green thread and again use this same thread to start the shading. Then carry on with the darker green and finally use the pale green for the veins. The stems are completed with the pale green. The barley heads are worked in 979. This completes the machine work.

Place a piece of extra heavy interfacing, the exact size of the box top card (K), behind the work, centralising the design. A triangle of pale green stitches fill the poppy centre and then three black bullion knots are worked. Straight stitches varying in length are added for the stamens which are completed by adding a small black seed bead at the end of each one.

Using a thread to match the background fabric, freely add more leaves and flower shapes in the background. As the fabric used for the box lining had a feint design, it was possible to outline it.

Remove the fabric from the frame and stretch the second piece. Trace and mark the fabric, as before, this time using the daisy design 16.2.

16.3 *An example of a barley head*

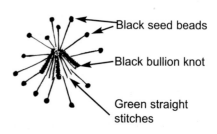

Black seed beads

Black bullion knot

Green straight stitches

16.4 *Stitching a poppy centre*

16.5 Poppies & Daisies embroideries

Daisies

Outline the daisy petals with the Gutermann white thread and fill in with the shiny white rayon thread.   (If the latter is not available, fill in with the ordinary white thread).

Outline the cornflowers with the darker blue and fill in with the paler blue. Outline and stitch the rounded leaves as before.   For the leaves with the serrated edge, use the brighter green followed by the darker and then the paler green. Stitch the stems as for the poppy design.   Work the background as before.

The daisy centres were made up of yellow French knots and yellow and gold beads. The centres of the cornflowers consisted of dark blue French knots and blue beads.

The two embroidered fabric pieces are now ready to be stretched onto the box top cards and stitched into position on the divided top napkin box.

17.   TABLE MATS BOX

The original for this box, using the orchard fruits fabric, was created for the table mats that Daphne uses.   Daphne had made a 'box with drawers' to contain coasters during the classes she took with Jackie at the very beginning of their friendship.   It seemed like a good idea to use some of the remaining fabric to make a matching box to take the table mats - these mats are circular with a diameter of 270mm.

Materials

2mm greyboard
½ metre of patterned cotton fabric for the outer covering
½ metre of co-ordinating cotton fabric for the inner lining
Strong thread for lacing
Sewing thread to match/tone with fabrics
Padding for lid

Equipment

Sharp pencil, set square and ruler
Cutting mat, sharp knife, and metal safety ruler
Scissors, pins and sewing needles
Fine, small curved needle

Preparation

For the base of the box, rule up and cut out pieces of card to the following dimensions.   Refer to page 5 for advice on this procedure.

A	Inside base	280mm x 280mm	1
B	Inner sides	280mm x 75mm	2
C	Inner sides	286mm x 75mm	2
D	Outer sides	286mm x 75mm	2
E	Outer Sides	292mm x 75mm	2
F	Outer Base	292mm x 292mm	1

For the lid, which has a dropped rim, cut the following pieces:

G	Inner base	295mm x 295mm	1
H	Inner sides	295mm x 26mm	2
I	Inner sides	301mm x 26mm	2
J	Outer sides	301mm x 30mm	2

| K | Outer sides | 307mm x 30mm | 2 |
| L | Lid top | 300mm x 300mm | 1 |

Method of construction

Identify the pieces of card for the box base according to the following diagram:

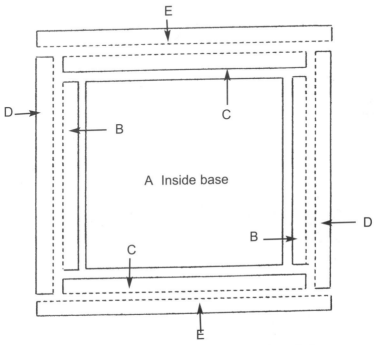

17.1   Bird's eye view of the carcass of the table mats box - the laced surfaces are indicated by dotted lines.

Cut out the appropriate fabric for each of the following pieces of card, allowing a margin of 20mm all round, and lace the fabric over the card.

A	Inside base	1	)	Lining
B	Inner sides	2	)	fabric
C	Inner sides	2	)	

D	Outer sides	2	)	Outer
E	Outer sides	2	)	fabric
F	Outer base	1	)	

Attach one covered side B, laced side outwards, to the covered base A, laced side downwards, using a matching sewing thread, ladder stitch with a curved needle, along the underside.   Stitch the second side B and the two sides C into place, in accordance with the bird's eye view diagram 17.1. Stitch down the corners using ladder stitch with a curved needle.

Position one covered side D in the correct place on the outside of the box, with the laced surface facing inwards, as shown in the diagram 17.1.   Stitch into position along all the edges, using ladder stitch with a curved needle. Stitch the second side D into position and then add the two covered sides E, stitching these in the same way.

Stitch the covered outer base F into position underneath the box, using ladder stitch with a curved needle, fitting the base exactly to the box.

Lid with drop sides

Cut the appropriate fabric, allowing a margin of 20mm all round, for the following pieces of card:

G	Lid lining	1	)	
H	Lining sides	2	)	Lining fabric
I	Lining sides	2	)	
J	Outer sides	2	)	
K	Outer sides	2	)	Outer fabric
L	Lid top	1	)	

Construct the lining section of the lid in exactly the same way as the inside base to the box, i.e. lacing the fabric over the appropriate pieces of card and stitching the lining sides to the lid lining.

The outer sides of the lid are deeper than the inner sides and, when stitching them into position, care should be taken to ensure that the lower edges are exactly flush, leaving the upper outer edges proud - the lid top is stitched into position inside these rising edges.

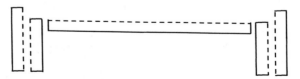

17.2   Creating the rim of the lid

18. TABLE MATS BOX WITH MACHINE QUILTING

The fruits and leaves design on this fabric was so pleasing that it was decided to simply quilt around the original design.

The patterned fabric was laid over a square of wadding, which was in turn placed over a cotton backing fabric.

The sandwich of fabrics was then tacked, on the patterned surface, to show the size of the finished lid and lines of tacking stitches were worked as a large diagonal cross from corner to corner to keep the fabrics in place.

Rather than quilt randomly, it was decided to confine the quilting to a circle, the outline of which was tacked on to the backing fabric.

The fruit shapes and leaves were then stitched round with back stitch using a fine Madeira gold metallic thread, following the gold outlines already present on the design.

Beads were then added, where the dots showing the shine on the berries were depicted, and also for the three areas of small berries, obviously meant to represent blackberries.

Around the edge of the circle, some of the fruits were not complete, so these were quilted over, which emphasised the circle.   As the surrounding fabric was left unstitched, it stands proud of the quilted area.

*The completed box
for the storage of table mats
and the lid top created by
quilting the fruit design fabric*

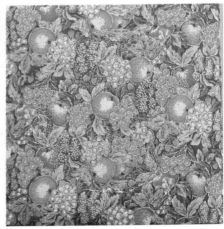

19. TABLE MATS BOX WITH CREATIVE EMBROIDERY

There are many lovely fabrics available, including those with an illusion of pattern rather than a definite design.   For this box, we have chosen such a fabric, which has shapes suggesting a sunflower.

The petal shapes were outlined in chain stitch and then emphasised by surrounding them with areas of French knots in a contrasting colour.   More shapes were then picked out and surrounded by chain stitch in a fine gold metallic thread.

Next, the remaining background areas were stitched, some in zigzag stitching which was worked on a machine. These areas could have been worked by hand, using back stitches.

Other areas were stitched by hand using straight stitches in groups of three, alternating the direction of each group.   Metallic thread was used for the background areas.

Throughout, the main stitching used Pearsall's filoselle embroidery silk and a Madeira fine gold metallic thread.

Beads were added to suggest the flower centre, in groups of six - a darker bead surrounded by five gold beads.

Look at the chosen fabric and decide which are the main pattern areas - use these for the coloured stitching.   For the other shapes, surround areas in pleasing sections, adding more lines and re-shaping areas if you think this would enhance the design.

Creative embroidery on box for storing place mats

Fabric chosen for the outer covering of the box

Finished lid top showing creative embroidery

20.   TALL TISSUES BOX

This tall square box with a circular aperture in the lid is intended as an outer holder for the upright tissues boxes.   The maximum size of a suitable box of tissues is 11 cm x 11 cm x 13.5 cm high.

Materials

2mm greyboard
½ metre of cotton or polycotton fabric
Strong thread for lacing
Sewing thread to match/tone with the fabric
Padding for lid

Equipment

Cutting mat, sharp knife and metal safety ruler
Plastic ruler and sharp pencil
Set square and pair of compasses
Scissors for fabric cutting
Usual sewing equipment
Fine curved needle
Needlework finisher and 10mm-wide double-sided adhesive tape

Method of Construction

Cut out pieces of 2mm greyboard to the following dimensions - see Page 5 for advice on the procedure:

S	Inside base	125mm x 125mm	1
T	Inner sides	125mm x 140mm	2
U	Inner sides	130mm x 140mm	2
V	Outer sides	130mm x 140mm	2
W	Outer sides	135mm x 140mm	2
X	Platform base	143mm x 143mm	1
Y	Lid	138mm x 138mm	1
Z	Lid lining	138mm x 138mm	1
Lid drops		138mm x 20mm	2
Lid drops		143mm x 20mm	2

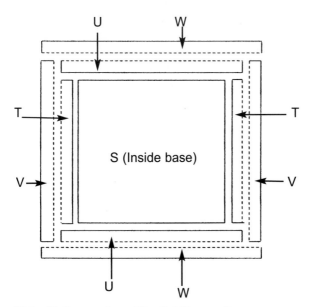

20.1   *Bird's eye view of the Tall Tissues Box carcass -*
the laced surfaces are indicated by dotted lines.

Allowing a margin of at least 20mm all round, cut pieces of fabric to cover each piece of card - S to U inclusive. Lace the fabric over the card.

Attach one covered side T, laced side outwards, to the covered base S, laced side downwards, using a matching sewing thread and ladder stitch, using a curved needle, along the underside.

Stitch the second side T and then the two sides U into place, in accordance with the bird's eye view diagram 20.1.   Stitch down the corners using ladder stitch with a curved needle.

Covering the outside of the box

Cut the fabric chosen for the outside of the box to cover the four side pieces V (2) and W (2), allowing 20mm turnings all round.   Lace each piece of fabric over the corresponding piece of card.

Position one covered side V in the correct place on the outside of the box, with the laced surface facing inwards, as shown in the bird's eye view diagram 20.1.   Stitch into position along all the edges, using ladder stitch with a curved needle.   Stitch the second side V into position and then add the two covered sides W, stitching these in the same way.

Platform Base:

Allowing a margin of 30mm all round, cut a piece of outer fabric to cover the platform base card X.   Lace the fabric over the card, keeping the lacing stitches well in from the edges so that they will not show when the box carcass is in position and taking special care with the mitred corners.

Place the carcass centrally on the covered platform base (laced surface uppermost) on a firm surface and pin securely into position.   Stitch the box carcass to the platform base, all round the lower edge of the carcass, using ladder stitch with a curved needle.

Lid with four drop sides

Mark a 75mm diameter circle centrally on card Y and and a 78mm. circle on card Z.   Using a Stanley knife, with a sharp blade, carefully cut out the circles and, if necessary, remove any rough edges with a sanding block.

Cut a piece of padding to the same dimensions as card Y.   Place the card on the padding and draw the outline of the circle on to the padding and cut this out.   Cut a piece of outer fabric to cover the card Y, allowing a margin of 20mm all round.   Place the card centrally on the wrong side of the fabric and draw the outline of the circle on the fabric.

Paint needlework finisher (or similar fray check) just inside the pencil line, allow to dry, and then cut out a circle of fabric 20mm inside this line, and cut up to the outline at intervals as shown in diagram 20.2 below.

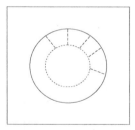

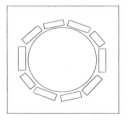

20.2   *Cutting out the circle of fabric in the centre of the aperture*

20.3   *Positioning the double-sided tape*

Position pieces of double-sided tape on the lid card Y all round the cut out panel as shown in diagram 20.3 above.

Place the outer fabric, right side down, on a firm surface with the padding in position on top and then the piece of card Y, lining up the circular holes.

Remove the paper from the double-sided adhesive tape and, pressing firmly downwards with one hand, with the other carefully pull the fabric evenly through the hole in the padding and card and press onto the adhesive tape.

Fold and pin the fabric over the outside edge on two opposite sides and lace between the outside edge and the fabric lining the aperture.   Lace the other pair of opposite sides.   Repeat the whole procedure for the lid lining card Z without the padding.

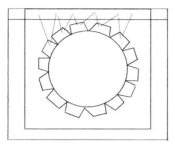

20.4   Lacing the fabric on the under-side of the lid

Lay the four drop side pieces of the lid in a line, the two longer pieces alternating with the other two.   Cut a piece of fabric twice the depth of the card plus a small seam allowance and position the cards on the outer covering fabric, right side down.

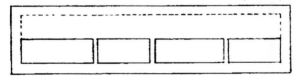

20.5   Card for lid drops positioned on the fabric

Fold the side edges in and the long edge down.   Pin the fabric tightly against the card and, either by hand using a back stitch or using the zip foot of a sewing machine, stitch the long seam tightly against the card.

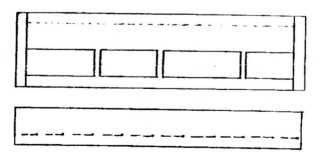

20.6   Folding the fabric over the card

After stitching, pull the fabric round the card until the seam is far enough down inside to allow for the covered lid card to rest on top and lie flush with the drops.

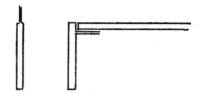

20.7   Moving the seam round to allow the lid card to fit in

Stitch the covered card Y in position flush with the lid drops, as shown in diagram 20.7 above, using ladder-stitch with a curved needle.

Position double-sided tape on the exposed card areas of the lid lining Z and, after removing the paper, position this card inside the lid (sandwiching the seam allowance of the drops) and hold firmly in position (or leave under a weight) for sufficient time to ensure that the surfaces are firmly fixed together.

Place a tall box of tissues, with its central card piece removed, inside the box. The lid will now fit snugly in position on the box and it should be possible to remove the tissues comfortably through the lid aperture.

20.8   Completed tall tissue box in poppy fabric

21. TALL TISSUES BOX WITH RIBBON ROSES

The embroidered roses which decorate the sides of the box were made using embroidery ribbon; however, satin ribbon or silk ribbon can, of course, be substituted for this.   Personal choice will dictate how the decorated panels are arranged on each side of the box.

Materials

¼ metre of fabric for the four outer panels of the box
3 shades of 4mm-wide pink embroidery ribbon
Pink Coton a Broder
Yellow Coton a Broder
3 shades of green stranded cotton - pale, medium & dark
Pale blue seed beads
Pale blue sewing thread
4 pieces of fine interfacing, the size of the card side panels

Equipment

7" circular wooden embroidery frame
Sharp embroidery scissors
No. 24 tapestry needle

Tracing paper
Sharp pencil
Embroidery needle

Preparation

Cut a piece of tracing paper the size of the card for the box sides.   Trace the circles for the three ribbon roses to give their position and cut them out. Stretch one of the pieces of fabric tightly in the frame and place the tracing over it.   Mark the positions of the cut-out circles lightly in pencil.

Embroidery

Using the pink thread, sew a series of seven straight stitches meeting at a central point to form the spokes of a wheel, in each of the spaces indicated in diagram 21.1 on page 92.

Bring a needle threaded with 3mm ribbon up in the centre of the wheel and begin to weave going round under and over the spokes. Pull the ribbon firmly at first and then more loosely towards the outside.   Work round as many times as needed to cover the spokes, then take the ribbon through to the back of the work and back stitch through the spokes on the reverse to finish off.   (See diagram 21.2.)

21.1 *Pattern for positioning the ribbon roses and suggestions for flowers*

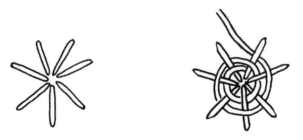

21.2 *Stages in working a woven rose*

The yellow French knots for the centre of the bead flowers are worked next. Add five blue beads evenly around the French knots.

Using the pale green thread, stem stitch the stem of the yellow French-knot flowers and then add some straight stitches at each side of the base of the stem.

Add the French knots.

Fans of straight stitches are now worked in the medium green thread.

To give depth to the embroidery, use the dark green thread to work French knots dotted around the centre of the work.

The work is now ready to be stretched. Place the fine interfacing onto the card and the fabric on top. Again use the pattern to ensure that the roses are in the correct place. Adjust the fabric as necessary. Turn over and lace the fabric in both directions.

Work the other three sides in the same way and assemble the box in accordance with the instructions for the tall tissues box..

21.3 Finished tall tissues box
with embroidered ribbon roses and hand embroidery

22. TALL TISSUES BOX LID WITH "COLOUR THROUGH GOLD"

The design for this embroidery is taken from a pack of ten designs by Daphne, using the centre section only.

Materials

8" square of Congress Cloth
Indian rayon threads - 1 cop each of: Pale Green
                                             Dark green
                                           Gold
                                           Red
1 reel of Madeira gold metallic thread No. 12, col. 33

Equipment

8" square wooden embroidery frame
No. 24 tapestry needle
Sharp embroidery scissors   Staples or drawing pins

Preparation

Stretch the Congress Cloth onto the frame, using either staples or drawing pins.   If drawing pins are used, it is advisable to cover the heads with masking tape to avoid the fine rayon threads catching on them.

Embroidery

Keep referring to the photographs, 22.1 and 22.3, for guidance as to the placing of the colours and the chart 22.2 for the direction of the stitches.

Mark the centre of the Congress Cloth and, starting at the centre, work a diagonal stitch over four threads in dark green.   Work eight more diagonal stitches on either side, diagonally over four threads (area marked D).

Work a similar area, again diagonally over four threads, in pale green - this shape sits inside the first shape.   Working from the corner of the large adjacent square, work a diagonal stitch over two threads in gold rayon thread.   Now work 18 more diagonal stitches on either side of this stitch to form the sides of the square.

This is followed by working diagonal stitches with the red rayon, this time over four threads, again with 18 on either side of the central stitch.

Still working towards the corner, work a diagonal stitch in gold rayon over two threads and 17 more diagonal stitches on either side, finishing with a single diagonal stitch over one thread.

Work a single cushion stitch square in metallic gold over eight threads (M on the chart). Working along the two unstitched sides of this square with gold rayon, stitch diagonally over two threads. Thread the needle with two red and one pale green thread, which should be doubled over to give six thicknesses, and this time work diagonally over four threads, bordering the previous gold stitches. Finally, to reach the outside of the square, work diagonally in gold rayon over two threads. Fill in the two triangular unstitched corners in dark green.

Having positioned the large square, work the remainder of the design, following the chart 22.2 and referring to the photographs 22.1 and 22.3. This will complete one quarter of the design. Turning the chart round 90o each time, complete the other three corners.

22.1 Finished "Colour through Gold" design for box top

22.2 *Chart for the top left quarter of the "Colour through Gold" design*

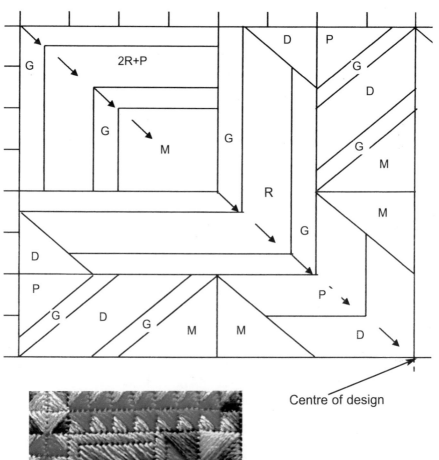

Centre of design

Shows direction
of stitches

22.3 *Enlargement of top
left-hand corner of
the design*

Key:	D	Dark green	P	Pale green
	G	Gold	R	Red
	M	Metallic gold	2R+P	2 Red & 1 Pale green

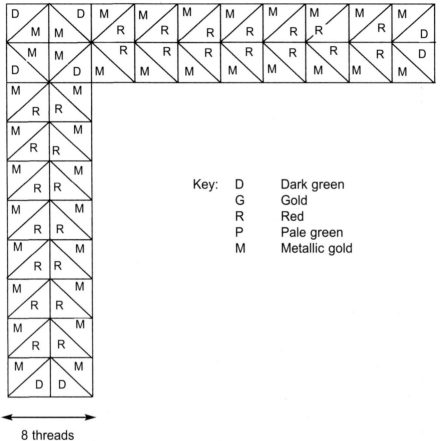

Key: D   Dark green
        G   Gold
        R   Red
        P   Pale green
        M   Metallic gold

8 threads

22.4   Border for the top left-hand quarter of the design

The border is worked over eight threads, using a complete cushion stitch in the centre of each side and for the four corners.   In between there are a series of five cushion stitches - note the direction of these (see 22.3).

Remember that, with a cushion stitch that is worked in two colours, the colour used for the centre stitch will have one more stitch than the corner colour.

23. BOX WITH TWO SMALL DRAWERS
AND LONG TOP TRAY WITH DIVISIONS

This rectangular box with two small drawers and a sectioned top tray area was designed specifically for the storage of lace bobbins in the drawers and the divisions in the top are for keeping threads, scissors and other items of equipment used in bobbin-lace making.   The lid and base are made flush with the outside of the box to make it easy to carry about without damaging the corners of the card.

Materials
2mm greyboard
½ metre each of the outer and inner fabrics
Strong thread for lacing
Sewing threads to match/tone with the fabrics
Padding for lid
Ribbons for lid stays, if required

Equipment
Cutting mat, sharp knife and metal safety ruler
Plastic ruler, sharp pencil and set square
Scissors for fabric cutting
Scissors, pins and sewing needles
Fine curved needle

23.1   Two-drawer box suitable for the storage of bobbin-lace equipment

23.2   Completed box showing top tray area

Method of construction

Rule up and cut out the following pieces of greyboard (see page 5 for advice about this) for one drawer and its casing and then cut a second set.

For the drawer:

A	Outer base	140mm x 140mm	1)	to be laced
B	Outer side panels	140mm x 40mm	2)	with outer
C	Outer front and back	145mm x 40mm	2)	fabric
D	Base lining for front & back	138mm x 37mm	2)	to be laced
E	Base lining sides	132mm x 37mm	2)	with lining
F	Base lining	132mm x 132mm	1)	fabric

For the casing:

G	Top and bottom	153mm x 148mm	2)	to be laced with
H	Sides	148mm x 43mm	3)	lining fabric

Cut out the fabric for each piece of card, allowing a 20mm margin all round, and lace the fabrics over the appropriate pieces of card.

<u>Tabs for drawer openings:</u>

The method to be used for opening the drawer should be decided now before the pieces of card are assembled and the front is attached to the base.

> Either 1.   Form a pull tab: make a narrow tube of fabric (or use ribbon) and stitch this to the centre of one of the laced surfaces of the covered base, where it will then be sandwiched as the front is stitched into position.

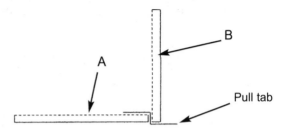

23.3   Ribbon or tube of fabric as it will be used as a pull tab

> or 2.   Stitch a button or other knob, as required, through the drawer-front, so that any fastening is on the laced surface, which will subsequently be hidden by the drawer lining.

<u>Making up the drawer base</u>

Attach the outer sides B, laced surfaces inwards, to the outer base A, laced surface uppermost, using a matching sewing thread, ladder stitch and a curved needle.   Stitch the front and back panels C into position in the same way (fitting across the two Bs) and ladder stitch down all the corners.

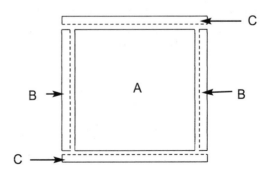

23.4   Bird's eye view of the outside of a drawer

Lining the drawer

Lace lining fabric over the front D and back D two sides E, and lining base F. Position the front and back inside the drawer and stitch along the top edges, using ladder stitch with a curved needle - see 23.5 below.

Position the side pieces and stitch these into place also along the top edges. The base F will now push-fit into place holding the sides in position. If required, the card surfaces of the lining and inner bases can be lightly glued and pressed together to hold the inner base permanently in position.

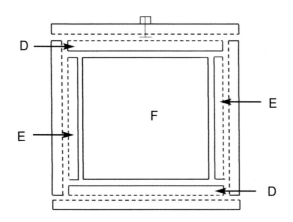

23.5   Bird's eye view of an assembled drawer
The laced surfaces are indicated by dotted lines.

Make a second drawer in the same way.

Assembling the casings

With the laced surfaces on the outside, stitch the top and bottom panels G and two of the side pieces H together, using ladder stitch with a curved needle, in accordance with diagram 23.6 below.

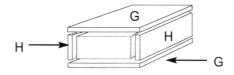

23.6   Arrangement of card for the drawer casing

Slide the drawer into the casing (this helps to stabilize it whilst stitching) and place the third covered side piece H in position, flush with the back of the casing, with the laced surface outside. Ladder stitch into place all round using a curved needle.

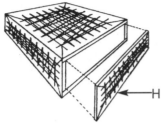

23.7 Inserting the back of the drawer casing

Once the two drawers and their casings have been assembled, the casings are ladder-stitched securely together, side by side.

Assembling the outer casing

For the outer casing pieces of the entire box: measure the outer areas of the sides and add 50mm to the height (to allow for the tray area required on top of the drawers) and add the width of a piece of fabric-covered card (3mm) to the depth. Cut two pieces of card to these dimensions and lace with outer fabric, allowing 20mm margins all round. With laced surfaces facing inwards, stitch these to the sides of the box, flush with the front of the drawer casings, using ladder stitch with a curved needle.

23.8 Outer casing pieces stitched into position and linings ready to be be assembled

For the box shown in the photograph 23.8 above, the measurements for the card for the outer casings, including the top layer, are:

Back	294mm x 110mm	1
Sides	143mm x 110mm	2
Front	294mm x 62mm	1

The top tray area can be designed according to personal choice.   To follow the suggested arrangement of the box shown in the photograph 23.2, cut the following pieces of card for the sections created inside the top layer:

Narrow inner section base	65mm x 131mm	1
Narrow long inner section sides	137mm x 59mm	2
Narrow short inner section sides	65mm x 59mm	2
Large inner section base	145mm x 132mm	1
Large long inner section sides	145mm x 59mm	2
Large short inner section sides	137mm x 59mm	2

Allowing a margin of 20mm all round, cut lining fabric to cover these pieces of card and then lace.   Ladder stitch the sides of the sections to their respective bases and then stitch the three sections together.

If stays are required to hold the lid open, choose ribbons or make these from the fabric.   Measure and stitch these into position at the required angle on the inside laced surface of the upper box area, allowing sufficient excess to be stitched behind the lining of the open lid.   If using two stays, make sure that the angles of the ribbons on either side are the same and the placings at identical distances from the back of the box.   (See diagram 25.4 on page 108 and photograph of the finished box 23.2.)

Make a hinge by doubling a piece of fabric and seaming it so that the finished size is 260mm x 40mm - check that this measurement is about 25mm shorter than the inside back edge of the box and adjust if necessary. Pin into position.

Put the three-section top tray into position and ladder-stitch around the top edges; be sure to stitch the hinge and the stays into place at the same time.

For the lid, lid lining and base, cut the following pieces of card and lace with the appropriate fabric, padding and embellishing the lid as required.   (Check that the dimensions given will fit the box before cutting the card.)

Lid and base (use greyboard)	145mm x 300mm	2
Lid lining (use thin card)	137mm x 284mm	1

Stitch the lid and lining into place, using the method described on page 15 and, if necessary, stitch the lid to the back of the box on the outside.
Lace the base card with outer fabric and ladder stitch into place underneath the box.

24.   "LACE BOBBINS" BOX WITH SHADED EMBROIDERY

For this box, a fabric was chosen with a poppy design.   This same fabric
may not be available when this book is published, so the following is a
description of how the design evolved from the fabric and similar ideas can
be used to develop designs from other floral patterned fabrics.

Look at the fabric and select flower and foliage shapes that are pleasing.
Trace these shapes.   For those that are too small, enlarge the tracings on a
photocopier.   For this box, three flower shapes were chosen and then a
selection of the foliage shapes - those coloured green and mauve.

24.1 Selection of flower and foliage shapes

These were then enlarged and the design was formed from a central poppy
and one on either side.   Then the poppies were surrounded by the foliage
shapes.   This was done by using a second piece of tracing paper and laying
it over the original piece and turning it until a pleasing design was achieved.
The central poppy was enlarged again and the foliage re-arranged.

24.2   Final design from the enlarged and arranged shapes

The design was then applied to the green background fabric by laying the tracing over the fabric and tacking the design outlines through the tracing paper and the fabric. The paper was then torn away leaving the design.

Split stitch along the outlines of the design using a double thread of stranded cotton - a medium green was used for the foliage, medium mauve for the mauve areas and medium cerise used for the flower petals. This stitching is covered by the first row of shading, giving a raised edge.

24.3   The finished embroidery to be stitched on to the lid

The long and short shading was worked with a single thread of Pearsall's filoselle embroidery silk, working from the outside of the flower petals with the palest shade and then continuing with the medium shade and finishing with the darkest shade.

The green foliage and mauve shapes were worked in a similar way and, finally, gold seed beads were added for the centres.

24.4
The finished
embroidery,
padded by a
layer of
extra heavy
interfacing,
laced over card
and stitched to
the lid of the
lace bobbins
box

25.   THREADS STORAGE BOX

This box is divided into four long sections, each of which is just the right size for the storage of the reels of threads used in making bobbin lace and could hold other items of equipment.   The large area of the lid is perfect for displaying embroidery or even lace and the lid is hinged.   The finished dimensions of the box are 280mm x 340mm x 50mm high.

Materials
2mm greyboard
1 metre each of the outer and inner fabrics
Strong thread for lacing
Sewing thread to match/tone with the fabrics
Padding for lid
Co-ordinating ribbon to use for the stays

Equipment
Sharp pencil, set square and ruler
Cutting mat, sharp knife and metal safety ruler
Fabric-cutting scissors
Scissors, pins and sewing needles
Fine curved needle

Cut out the following pieces of card, referring to page 5 for advice on this procedure.

Inner section bases	330mm x 60mm	4
Long inner section sides	335mm x 40mm	8
Short inner section sides	60mm x 40mm	8
Long outer sides	335mm x 50mm	2
Short outer sides	270mm x 50mm	2
Outer base	335mm x 265mm	1
Lid	340mm x 275mm	1
Lid lining	330mm x 265mm	1

The pieces of card that will be required to make up each of the four base sections of the box are shown in diagram 25.1 below:

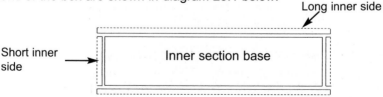

25.1   Bird's eye view of one section of the threads box.
The laced surfaces are indicated by the dotted lines

Method of construction
Allowing a margin of 20mm all round, cut lining fabric for each of the pieces of card needed to make up the inner sections.   Lace each piece of fabric over the appropriate card.

Attach one short covered side, laced side outwards, at right angles to the covered inner base, laced side downwards, using a matching sewing thread, ladder stitch and a curved needle, along the underside.

Stitch the second short side and the two long sides into place, in accordance with diagram 25.2.   Stitch down the corners using ladder stitch with a curved needle.

Make up all four sections in a similar way.   Now join the four together, using ladder stitch with a curved needle, to stitch the top and lower edges of the long sides together.

25.2   Constructing the inner sections of the threads storage box

Covering the outside of the box
Cut the fabric chosen for the outside of the box to cover the outer base card, allowing a margin of 20mm all round, and lace this.   Place the card, laced side uppermost, on a flat surface, and position the four sections on top, which should lie flush.   Using ladder stitch and a curved needle, stitch all round to attach the base to the sections.

Allowing 30mm turnings all round, cut outer fabric to cover the four outer side pieces of card,.   Lace each piece of fabric over the corresponding piece of card, arranging the fabric on the laced side so that it comes more than 10mm over one long side - this is to allow for the outer sides of the box to rise above the linings - see diagram 25.3 on following page.

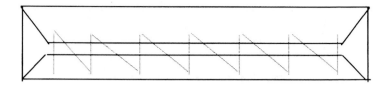

25.3   Lacing arrangement for the outer sides of the threads storage box

If the opening of the box lid is to be restrained by a stay or stays, these need to be put in position at this stage.

Photograph 25.6 on page 110 shows a threads box under construction with two stays holding the lid open.   For this purpose, use a co-ordinating ribbon or make a narrow band from the fabric being used for the lining of the box.

The ribbons should be stitched in place at the required angle on the laced surface of the shorter sides of the carcass of the box, allowing sufficient excess to be stitched behind the lining of the open lid.   If using two stays, make sure that the angles of the ribbons on either side are the same and the placings at identical distances from the back of the box.

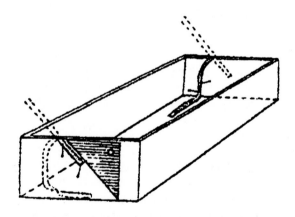

25.4   Positioning stays on the outside of the box carcass.
The excess ribbon is stitched between the lid and its lining.

Position one of the long outer sides in the correct place on the outside of the box, laced side inwards, as shown in the bird's eye view diagram 25.5 opposite, so that the bottom edge of the card is flush with the base of the carcass.   Stitch into position along all the edges, using ladder stitch with a curved needle.

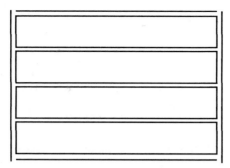

*25.5   Bird's eye view of the threads storage box with four sections
and the outer sides of the box in position*

Constructing the hinge

Cut a piece of outer fabric approximately 330mm x 100mm.   Fold this in
half longways, right sides together, seam across the ends, turn and press.

Stitch the hinge to the laced side of the remaining long outer side, leaving
30mm of the hinge standing proud of the box.   Stitch this outer side into
position, stitching the hinge in at the same time.   Add the two shorter sides
stitching these in the same way.

Lid

Cut a piece of padding to the exact dimensions of the lid card. Next,
allowing a margin of 30mm all round, cut a piece of outer fabric to cover the
lid card.   If any embroidery or decoration is to be applied to the lid, this
should be carried out at this stage.

Place the fabric on a firm surface, wrong side uppermost, position the
padding centrally and then the piece of lid card on top.

Pin one pair of opposite sides of the lid fabric, pulling the fabric firmly and
evenly to remove any creases, and lace, keeping the lacing stitches well in
from the edges.   Pin and lace the other two sides, mitring the corners
carefully as these will be visible.

Cut a piece of lining fabric to cover the lining card, allowing a margin of
20mm all round, and lace the fabric over the card.

Stitch the lid and lining into position following the instructions given in the
Basic Techniques section on page 15.

25.6 Lid, with stays, hinged in position on base and waiting for the lid lining

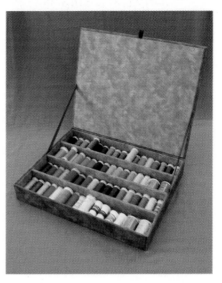

25.7 Finished threads storage box filled with Gutermann threads

26.1 Threads storage box decorated with shaded embroidery roundels based on the fabric design

26. THREADS STORAGE BOX WITH SHADED EMBROIDERY

The glorious fabric used to cover this box for the storage of reels of threads is the inspiration for the two roundels of long and short stitch shaded embroidery which have been applied to the lid.

Materials

Two 8" squares of pale green cotton lining fabric
Two 3½" circles of Vilene extra heavy interfacing
Two 3½" circles of mounting card

Pearsall's filoselle embroidery silk - 1 skein each of:

Willow green	255
Grass green	104
Grass green	102
Rose	085
Brick red	305
Orange yellow	150
Scarlet	021
Maize gold	097A
White	088

Stranded cotton - small amounts of dark brown, tan
and three shades of yellow

Sewing cotton to match the lining fabric

Equipment

6" circular wooden embroidery frame
Fine embroidery needle
Sharp embroidery scissors
Tracing paper
Sharp pencil

Preparation

Stretch one of the squares of lining fabric onto the circular frame. Trace the nasturtium flower and leaves design (26.2) and place the tracing behind the fabric and draw the design onto it with a sharp pencil.

26.2   Design for nasturtium and leaves

Embroidery - Nasturtium

Using two strands, back stitch around the flower petals in the white silk and around the leaves in the palest green.

Start the long and short stitch shading on the flower with a single strand of the white silk, taking the stitches over the back stitched edges.

Carry on with the shading using maize gold 097A, scarlet 021 and rose 085. Refer to the photograph 26.3 for the positioning of the colours.

Work seven small bullion knots radiating from the flower centre and then work small maize gold stitches in between them.

Using a single strand, back stitch the veins of the leaves with the palest green and, still using this silk, start the long and short stitch shading around the outside.

Continue the shading using the medium green and finally the darkest green. Whip the veins with the palest green silk.

*Place one circle of interfacing centrally behind the design and, using the matching sewing thread, back stitch around the embroidered areas as indicated by the dotted lines.

Gather around the outside of the design about ½" away from the outside edge of the interfacing.

Remove the work from the frame.   Place one of the card circles behind the interfacing, pull up the gathering thread and fasten off.

Lace across the back of the circle to ensure the embroidery is well stretched.*

26.3   Shaded embroidery nasturtium roundel

<u>Embroidery - Helenium</u>

Stretch the second piece of lining fabric onto the frame.   Mark the design
26.4 onto the fabric as for the nasturtium.

Using two threads, back stitch around the flower petals in rose 085, around
the flower centre in one of the yellow stranded cottons and around the
leaves using the darkest green, always .

The shading is all worked in a single strand of the silk.   Begin with the rose
085, using long and short stitches, which go over the back-stitched edging.
Carry on with the shading using brick red 305 and orange yellow 156.

The lower part of the flower centre is filled with French knots tightly packed
together, which are worked using one strand each of the three yellow
stranded cottons.

26.4 Design for helenium and leaves

26.5   Shaded embroidery helenium roundel

The top part of the flower centre is worked again with French knots but using one strand of dark brown and one strand of tan stranded cotton. Satin stitch the flower stem using a single strand of the darkest green.

Back stitch the leaf veins in the darkest green and, still using this silk, start the long and short stitch shading around the outside of the leaf.   Complete the shading with the medium and palest greens.   Whip the veins in the darkest green.

Assemble as for the nasturtium, working from * to *.

The two roundels are now ready to be attached to the box top using ladder stitch with a curved needle.

27.   OCTAGONAL BOX FOR STORING CRAFT TOOLS

The divisions in this eight-sided box make it ideal for transporting craft tools. The box does not have a hinged lid and the base is fitted smoothly to the box, so as to avoid the card corners being damaged as it is carried about.

Materials

2mm greyboard
½ metre each of the outer and lining fabrics
Strong thread for lacing
Sewing thread to match/tone with the fabrics
Padding for the lid and the outside of the carcass

Equipment

Sharp pencil, set square and plastic ruler
Cutting mat, sharp knife and metal safety ruler
Fabric cutting scissors
Sharp scissors, pins and sewing needles
Fine curved needle

Method of construction

Cut out the octagonal base card (following the advice given on page 5) in accordance with diagram 27.1, the dimensions of which are:

240mm long outer edges
100mm short outer edges
60mm angled edges

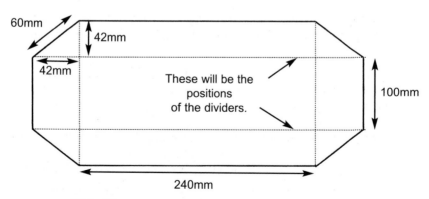

27.1   *Dimensions of the base of the octagonal box*

Cut rectangles to form the sides of the box, each of which is 60mm high:

Long sides	240mm x 60mm	2
Short sides	100mm x 60mm	2
Angled sides	60mm x 60mm	4

Allowing a margin of 20mm all round, cut out and lace lining fabric over the octagonal base and the eight side pieces of card.

Put each side piece, unlaced surface to unlaced surface with the appropriate edge of the octagonal base and oversew the pieces together - see pages 7 and 8. Once all the sides have been stitched in place, stitch each side piece to its neighbour, forming an eight-sided box.

For the dividers, cut two pieces of card 324mm x 57mm. Each piece needs to be entirely covered with lining fabric in such a way that it can be used to divide the box.

Cut out fabric to twice the depth of the card plus a margin of 20mm all round.

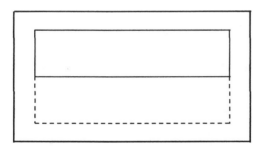

27.2 Cut card for a divider positioned on the fabric - dotted area indicates that twice the depth of the card must be allowed for.

Before folding the fabric down and stitching, lay two or three pieces of strong thread along the length of the divider with several inches protruding on either side.

27.3 Positioning the threads prior to folding the fabric down for stitching

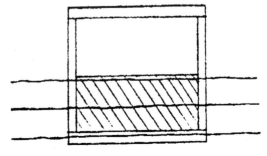

117

Fix the dividers in position, by using a strong needle to pass the protruding threads through the joins in the sides of the box carcass, and tie the ends off firmly.

Covering the outside of the box

Cut a 60mm-wide strip of padding to go around the outside of the carcass and trim so that the ends butt together.   Remove the padding from the carcass and stitch the ends together so that it lies flat.   Replace the padding around the carcass.

27.4   Butting the ends of the padding so that it will lie flat

Cut a strip of outer fabric 100mm wide and long enough to go right around the outside of the carcass and overlap by 50mm.   Place the strip, right side to the padding, around the outside and pin the ends together.   Remove from the box and pin again 5mm inside the original pin line and stitch (by hand or machine) along this new line and press open.

Remove the padding from the box.   Take the prepared outer covering and stand it inside the box, the right way up and right side out, positioning the join at one of the back seams.

Fold the cover over the top edge of the box so that approx. 20mm extend down the outside of the box and pin into place along the top edge of the box - it may be necessary to "ease" the material to lose any slight surplus.

With a thread chosen to match/tone with the lining and/or outer fabric, sew the outer cover to the base along the top outer edge with small even stitches.   Take care to catch the lining material underneath - have a look underneath occasionally to check that this is being achieved.   Aim to make stitches sufficiently small and evenly spaced that they will be almost invisible when the cover is turned out.

27.5   Angle of the needle
when stitching the
outer cover
into position

Replace the padding and turn the cover out over the padding to the outside of the box. Pull the covering fabric down over the padding and take care not to move or wrinkle the padding in the process. Pull the material to the underside of the box (checking that it is pulled evenly) and pin into position. If necessary, smooth out any wrinkles in the padding before pinning and lacing the fabric underneath the box.

Finished octagonal box carcass

Cut out three pieces of octagonal card, one for the base, one for the lid (these are the same size) and the other for the lid lining. Cut outer fabric for the lid card (30mm margin), and for the base card (20mm margin) and lining fabric for the lid lining. Lace the fabrics over the appropriate cards, padding the lid if required. Ladder stitch the base card underneath the box. Ladder stitch the lid lining, centrally, to cover the lacing on the underside of the lid.

27.7
Dimensions
for the card for
lid and base

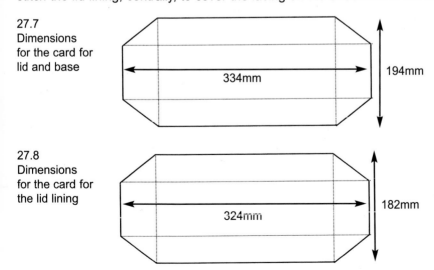

334mm

194mm

27.8
Dimensions
for the card for
the lid lining

324mm

182mm

28.   OCTAGONAL BOX WITH EMBROIDERED COCKEREL ON LID

The fabric chosen for the outer covering of the box depicts scenes in a hen house and a single cockerel was chosen for the embroidery on the lid, which was worked in simple embroidery stitches using Pearsalls silks.

Materials

Pearsall's filoselle silk embroidery thread:

1 skein each of:	Silver grey	144 & 146
	White	088
	Marigold	179, 182 & 183
Small quantities of:	Goblin green	129 & 131
	Bark brown	169
	Old gold	121
	Red/scarlet	162

A piece of card cut to fit on the lid, appropriate for the finished embroidery
Lining fabric large enough to cover the cut card
Coton a Broder or similar thread - Straw gold
Matching sewing cotton - Straw coloured
Extra heavy interfacing - cut to the size of the card
1 dark bead for cockerel eye   Beading thread

Equipment

10" circular wooden embroidery frame   Tracing paper & sharp pencil
Fine embroidery needle   Sharp embroidery scissors
                                                                       Beading needle

Preparation

Stretch the fabric tightly into the frame.   Trace the design and lay the tracing over the fabric and tack along the design lines.   Remove the tracing paper, leaving the tacked design.

Embroidery

This is all worked using a single strand of the silk (with the exception of the grain in the bowl).   The colours and stitches used are marked on the diagram opposite 28.1.

The tail feathers have a central line of stem stitch and are then completed with sloping straight stitches.   Directly above these large feathers are the finer ones which are worked in rows of stem stitch using 179, 182 and 183.

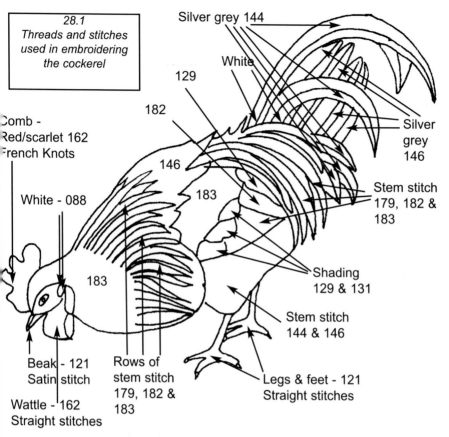

28.1
Threads and stitches
used in embroidering
the cockerel

Silver grey 144

White

129

182

Silver
grey
146

Comb -
Red/scarlet 162
French Knots

146

183

Stem stitch
179, 182 &
183

White - 088

183

Shading
129 & 131

Stem stitch
144 & 146

Beak - 121
Satin stitch

Rows of
stem stitch
179, 182 &
183

Legs & feet - 121
Straight stitches

Wattle - 162
Straight stitches

28.2   *Finished hand-embroidered cockerel*

The under body uses the two greys and stem stitch, which is worked in swirls. The small back areas are worked as marked on the diagram.

The neck feathers are also worked in rows of stem stitch in 179, 182 and 183.

The facial features are as shown on the drawing 28.1. Keep looking at the photograph 28.2 of the finished embroidery which will help you.

The comb is worked in French knots and the wattle in straight stitches.

The beak, legs and feet are worked in satin stitch.

The bowl holding the grain is worked in long and short stitch using 129.

The grain is worked in two strands - one of 169 and one of 121 - using French knots.

The straw is represented by two straw gold threads of Coton a Broder which is couched on using the matching colour sewing thread.

Cut the extra heavy interfacing exactly to the size and shape of the card and then stretch the embroidered fabric over both the interfacing and card - centralising the embroidery - and lace.

Ladder stitch the embroidered panel onto the lid of the box.

28.3 Finished octagonal box with cockerel on padded lid

29.1   The "bee" box, which is covered with stumpwork bees
and the side panels are alternately fabric and
"Colour through Gold" embroidery

29. HEXAGONAL BOX WITH "COLOUR THROUGH GOLD" AND STUMPWORK BEES

This is a "novelty" box, octagonal and embellished with stumpwork bees and Colour through Gold "honeycomb" embroidery on three of the side panels. The remaining side panels are covered with a bee fabric and the lining to the box is a honeycomb fabric.

The "Colour through Gold" panels

Materials

10" square of Congress Cloth
1 reel of Madeira Gold metallic thread No. 12, col. 33
One cop each of Indian rayon thread in: Deep Yellow
                                            Pale Yellow
                                            Tan
3 panels of 2mm greyboard, each 112mm high x 89mm wide
3 pieces of lining fabric to lace over the greyboard - allow 20mm margin
1 yard of gold ribbon 7mm wide
Petite gold beads

Equipment

10" square wooden frame   Sharp embroidery scissors
No. 24 tapestry needle   Staples or drawing pins
Beading needle   Sharp pencil

Preparation

Staple or drawing pin the Congress Cloth on to the frame; if drawing pins are used, cover the heads with masking tape to avoid the threads catching on them. Divide the square into three rectangles, each approximately 3" x 4", and lightly mark the centre of each rectangle with a pencil.

Embroidery

Throughout the work, use the rayon threads in six thicknesses (three threads through the needle, doubled) and a single gold metallic thread through the needle and doubled.

Start by working the grid in the gold metallic thread - the horizontal stitches are each over six threads of the Congress Cloth - repeating the sequence of stitches, until the panel has the same number of shapes as photograph 29.3.

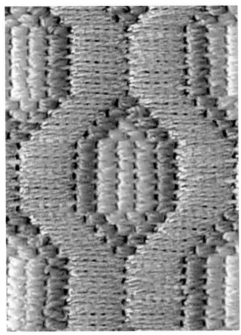

29.2
Central area of
"Colour through
Gold" design on the
side panels

Fill in each of the hexagonal shapes with horizontal stitches over two threads, with tan outlining the shape, then deep yellow and the pale yellow in the centre.

29.3   One of the three
embroidered side panels for
the hexagonal Bee box.

The completed panel is
shown surrounded by
gold ribbon,
which has been attached to
a piece of lining fabric using
petite gold beads

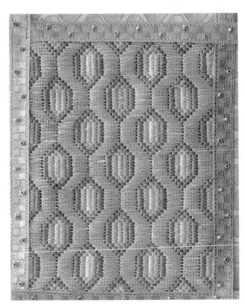

Repeat the design in the other two rectangles.

Stitch each of the "Colour through Gold" panels onto the piece of the lining fabric cut out to cover the card for the outside of the box. Outline each with gold ribbon, which is stitched into place with the petite gold beads.

Lace each over the piece of cut card and use as directed in constructing the outside of the box.

Materials for the box

2mm greyboard	Strong thread for lacing
½ metre bee fabric	Sewing thread to match/tone with fabrics
¼ metre lining fabric	

Equipment

Sharp pencil, set square and plastic ruler
Pair of compasses
Cutting mat, sharp knife and metal safety ruler
Scissors, pins and sewing needles
Fine curved needle

Method of construction

For the base of the box, cut the following card pieces - see page 5 for advice on this procedure:

Outer side panels	112mm high x 94mm wide	6
Inner side panels	112mm high x 89mm wide	3
Hexagonal inner base	178mm diameter	1
Hexagonal Platform base	215mm diameter	1

Allowing a margin of 20mm all round, cut lining fabric to cover each of the inner side panels and the hexagonal inner base and lace. Oversew, right sides facing, the side panels to the base and then stitch each side to its adjacent panel - page 8 gives advice about this procedure.

Allowing a margin of 20mm all round, cut bee fabric to cover the outer side panels, , and lace the fabric over the card.   Using ladder stitch and a curved needle, stitch each of the six outer panels in turn (taking the bee fabric and embroidered panels alternately) to the base of the box.

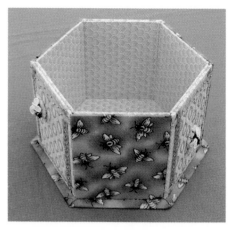

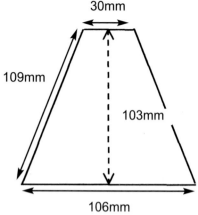

30mm

109mm

103mm

106mm

29.4 Base of hexagonal Bee Box   *29.5 Side panel for lid of box*

Cut bee fabric to cover the platform base, allowing a margin of 30mm all round, and lace over the card.   Place the box carcass on the platform base, laced surface uppermost, and stitch into position using ladder stitch and a curved needle.

For the lid of the box, cut the following card pieces:

Hexagonal lid lining	194mm diameter	1
Side panels	see diagram 29.5 above	6
Top hexagon	60mm diameter	1

Allowing a margin of 20mm all round, cut bee fabric to cover the six side panels of the lid.   Lace the fabric over the pieces of card but take care to keep the lacing stitches well away from the longer lower edge.   Using ladder stitch with a curved needle, stitch the long sides of the panels together side by side.

Allowing a margin of 20mm all round, cut out lining fabric to cover the larger hexagonal lid lining card and lace the fabric over the card.   With the laced surface inside, push this into position, evenly, inside the lid - there will be a lip showing of approximately 10mm.   Using ladder stitch and a curved needle, stitch the lining into position.

The 60mm diameter hexagon is to provide a mount for the Queen Bee, the instructions for which follow in the next section.

The Stumpwork Bees

Materials

2 x 10" squares of crystal chiffon
2 x 10" squares of cotton backing
2 x 10" squares of lining fabric
Sewing cotton to match the lining
Stranded cotton - white, black and gold
Fine silver metallic thread
Black Nymo D beading thread
Black seed beads
10 white cake wires No. 28
Extra heavy interfacing - sufficient to cut out 10 x 10p-piece shapes and
                                              one piece 60mm diameter

Equipment

8" wooden circular embroidery frame
Sharp embroidery scissors
Embroidery needle
Fine curved needle
Beading needle
Large needle (to make the holes to put the wire through)
Old scissors to cut the wire

Embroidery

Stretch the cotton backing with the chiffon on top
into the frame.   Take a cake wire and bend it to
the shape shown in diagram 29.6 to make a pair
of wings.   With a single strand of white stranded
cotton, couch the wire on from X to X.   (This
leaves the ends free to go through the fabric.)

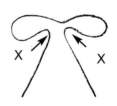

29.6   Wings for the bees

Blanket stitch round, again using a single strand, going over the wire and
through the fabric.   With the silver thread, starting at the tip of each wing,
feather stitch to the centre.   Cut out carefully close to the blanket stitch
edging.

Each bee requires two sets of wings.   The featured box has ten bees on it.
Decide on the number required and make two sets of wings per bee.

Remove the fabric from the frame and put the lining fabric onto it.

Queen Bee   Small bees

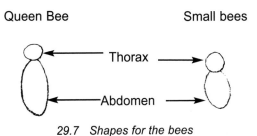

29.7   Shapes for the bees

Using the bee shape, outline as many bee shapes as required in back stitch.

Starting at the lower edge, work turkey knots in the abdomen: work three rows in black, two rows in gold, two rows in black, two rows in gold and then complete with black.   Cut the loops and trim the threads to shape.

Second set

Holes for first
set of wings

*29.8   Positioning
the wings*

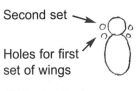

Push the wires of one pair of wings into the lower two holes.   The second pair go into the upper holes.   Attach to the fabric with black thread coming up at the top of the abdomen and going down at the top of the thorax.   Use about five stitches.   Immediately above the thorax, stitch on two black beads and then add a single stitch to part the beads.   Catch the wires down behind the body, folding the wires over to make a loop - stitch into the loop to ensure they do not move.

Using a 10p piece, draw a circle for each bee on the extra heavy interfacing and cut out.   Place these centrally over circles of lining fabric and run a gathering thread around the fabric about ¼" away from the interfacing.   Cut the lining fabric outside the gathering thread.   Gather up and stitch from side to side to stretch the fabric over the interfacing.

Stitch a bee to each circle and then stitch these in position on the box and lid.   Stitch the circles onto the box using a curved needle.

For the Queen Bee, cut a circle of interfacing with 60mm diameter and cut to hexagon shape for top of lid. Follow the same procedure as for the worker bees and stitch to top of lid.

*29.9
The Queen
Bee on the
lid top*

30.   LARGE TISSUES BOX WITH OVAL APERTURE

The design for this tissue box is based on the boxes of tissues sold as being "man-sized" but which are, in fact, eminently suitable for use by everyone, especially those suffering from a cold!

Materials
2mm greyboard
Thinner card for lid lining
½ metre of patterned cotton fabric for outer covering
½ metre of plain cotton fabric for the lining
Strong thread for lacing
Sewing thread to match/tone with fabrics
Padding for the lid (optional)

Equipment
Sharp pencil, set square and ruler
Cutting mat, sharp knife and metal safety ruler
Scissors, pins and sewing needles
Fine curved needle   Double-sided adhesive tape
Fray check (optional)

Preparation
Measure and cut out the greyboard to the following dimensions, following the advice for this procedure given on page 5:

A	Inside base	165mm x 315mm	1
B	Inner sides	165mm x 55mm	2
C	Inner sides	321mm x 55mm	2
D	Outer sides	171mm x 65mm	2
E	Outer sides	327mm x 65mm	2
F	Outer Base	321mm x 171mm	1
G	Lid	321mm x 171mm	1

From thin card, cut a lid lining: H   312mm x 162mm   1

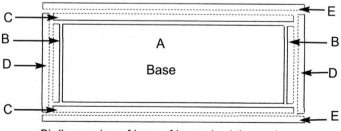

Bird's eye view of base of large-sized tissues box

Method of construction

Cut out lining fabric, allowing a margin of 20mm all round, to cover A, B (2) and C (2), and lace the fabric over the card. Using ladder stitch with a curved needle, stitch the side pieces to the base at right angles, laced surfaces on the outside.

Cut the fabric chosen for the outer cover, allowing a margin of 20mm all round, to cover D (2), E (2) and F and lace the fabric over the card. Using ladder stitch with a curved needle, stitch the side pieces to the base at right angles, as for the inner box, but with the laced surfaces on the inside.

Place the lining box inside the outer box, pressing it firmly down. Using ladder stitch with a curved needle, stitch the lining into place along the top edges - the lining will be lower than the outer, to allow for the lid to drop neatly into the box and rest on the lining.

Mark a suitable oval shape on the lid card, carefully cut out the shape and, if necessary, remove any rough edges with a sanding block . Position pieces of double-sided tape on the lid card all round the cut out panel (see diagram 20.3 on page 88) and along the outer edges.

Cut a piece of padding to the same dimensions as the lid card G. Place the card on the padding and draw the outline of the oval on to the padding and cut this out. Allowing a margin of 25mm all round, cut a piece of outer fabric to cover the card G, . Place the card centrally on the wrong side of the fabric and draw the outline of the oval on the fabric.

If desired, paint needlework finisher (or similar fray check) just inside the pencil line and allow to dry. Cut out an oval of fabric 20mm inside the pencil line, and cut up to the outline at intervals.

Place the outer fabric, right side down, on a firm surface with the padding in position on top and then the piece of thick card G, lining up the oval holes. Remove the paper from the double-sided adhesive tape and, pressing down firmly on the card, carefully pull the fabric evenly through the hole in the padding and card and press onto the adhesive tape.

Remove the paper from the tape on the outer edges and carefully fold the fabric over the outside edges and press into place. Repeat the whole procedure for the lid lining card H, marking a slightly smaller oval and without the padding. Put the laced surfaces of the lid and lining together (lining up the oval cut-outs) and ladder stitch together, using a curved needle.

31. LARGE-SIZE TISSUES BOX LID WITH RIBBON FLOWERS & BEADS

31.1   Lid of tissue box showing ribbon embroidery

A floral fabric was chosen for the covering of the outside of this box to give the opportunity to embellish the lid with ribbon and beads.   This particular fabric may no longer be available but, from the steps which follow, it should be possible to adapt the idea for other flower fabrics.   (For help with the stitching techniques, see page 136 in the Stitch Glossary.)

For the foliage, the idea was to give depth to the design so areas were chosen to remain as background and these were not stitched.

The middle distance foliage was selected and this was outlined and the veins were stitched.

The most pleasing and largest leaves were fully stitched with long and short stitch shading. Finally a few ribbon leaves were added around the ribbon flowers and these became part of the foreground.

Similarly, some flowers were selected to be embroidered, leaving the unstitched ones to form part of the background.   The side flowers were shaded with long and short stitches and given French knot centres.

The flowers to be embellished with gathered ribbons were then selected and worked, balancing the colours across the lid.   These also had bead centres worked in two colours.

Finally, daisy type flowers were added to complete the embroidery and these were worked by actually stitching with the ribbon and then they were given French knot centres.

Pearsall's filoselle silk thread was used for the embroidery and embroidery ribbon for the ribbon flowers but these could, of course, be worked in silk ribbon.   No. 11 seed beads formed the ribbon flower centres.

31.2 Finished large tissue box with ribbon embroidery

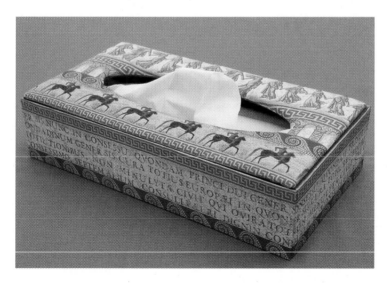

31.3 Large tissue box made up in an interesting Greek-style fabric

<u>STITCH GLOSSARY</u>

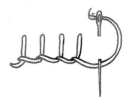

Blanket Stitch

Bullion knot

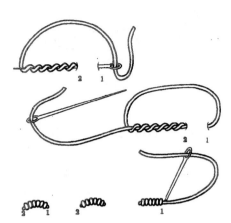

Chain Stitch

Couching

Four-sided stitch

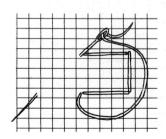

```
      3
D ——→ B        Stitch in the order:
↑        ↑           A to B
4|      |1           C to A
C ——→ A         D to B and
      2              C to D
```

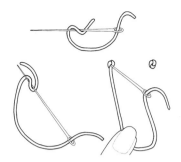

French knot

Long & Short Stitch

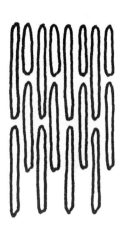

Needle Lace

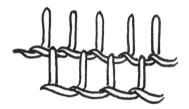

Rhodes Stitch over eight threads

 - note that the final stitch, 33 to 34, repeats stitch 1 to 2 but in the opposite direction, i.e on top of stitch 1 to 2.

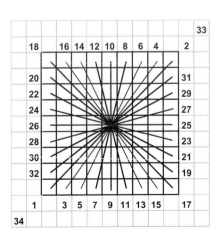

Gathered ribbon petal:

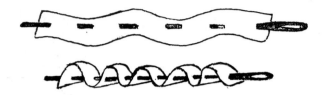

Cut 3mm ribbon into 1¼" lengths. Bring needle containing matching colour cotton up through the fabric and put the needle down in the middle of the ribbon 3mm from one end. Gather the ribbon onto the needle as shown in the diagram.

Put the needle back through its first entry point in the ribbon and back through the fabric, ensuring that the ribbon ends are one on top of the other. As it is pulled through the fabric, the ribbon will gather to make the petal - secure on the reverse with a back stitch.

Stitching with ribbon

When working with ribbon in the needle, it is best to stitch with 'soft' ribbons - silk or 100% polyester. Practice guiding the ribbon with the forefinger of the free hand to prevent it twisting - it is easier to prevent the twists, rather than try to straighten them out later! Use a tapestry needle for this technique.

Half daisies in ribbon

Formed by stitching fans of irregular length straight stitches, all appearing to come from a central point.

Full daisies in ribbon

Formed using straight stitches - to allow for perspective, the stitches at the rear should be shorter than those in the foreground.

The centres are filled with French knots or beads.

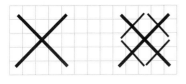

Rice Stitch

Satin Stitch

Split Stitch

Stem Stitch

Turkey Knot

Holding the thread on top of the fabric, take the needle down at A1 and come up at B1 - stage 1. Take the thread over the top of A1 and go down at C1, bringing the needle up again at A1 - stage 2. Pull the thread down firmly and make a downwards loop.

Holding the loop, take the needle down at a new point just to the right of the previous stitch and repeat the procedure.

Stage 1

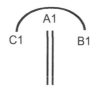

Stage 2

Whipped Back Stitch

Zig Zag Back Stitch

Index to Embroidery Techniques used

Suppliers

G J Beads

Unit 1-3, Court Arcade
The Wharf
ST. IVES, Cornwall
TR26 1LG
Tel/Fax: 91736 793886
email: Beadyspice@aol.com
www.GJBEADS.co.uk

Pauline's Patchwork
(fabrics)

Brewers Quay
Hope Square
WEYMOUTH, Dorset
DT4 8TP
Tel: 01305 766543

Pearsall's Embroidery Silks
(silk threads used in
projects: 3, 9, 17, 18
23, 25, 27 & 30)

Tancred Street
TAUNTON
Somerset TA1 1RY
Tel: 01823 274700

Stitches of Halifax
(fabrics)

69 Caldene Avenue
Mytholmroyd
Nr Hebden Bridge, HALIFAX
HX7 5AJ
Tel: 01422 884699